SANTA FE
in a Week
(more or less)

PORTS OF CALL™ BOOK SERIES
www.portsofcallbooks.com
A VIRTUAL IMPRINT OF THE BOOK MARKETING GROUP™

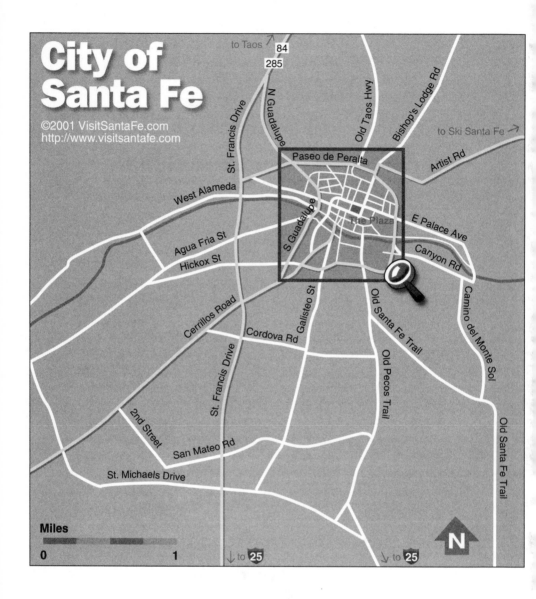

City of Santa Fe

to Taos 84 285

N Guadalupe

St. Francis Drive

Old Taos Hwy

Bishop's Lodge Rd

to Ski Santa Fe

Artist Rd

Paseo de Peralta

West Alameda

S Guadalupe

The Plaza

E Palace Ave

Agua Fria St

Hickox St

Canyon Rd

Camino del Monte Sol

Cerrillos Road

Galisteo St

Cordova Rd

Old Santa Fe Trail

St. Francis Drive

Old Pecos Trail

Old Santa Fe Trail

2nd Street

San Mateo Rd

St. Michaels Drive

Miles

0   1

to 25   to 25

N

SANTA FE
in a Week
(more or less)

A GUIDE TO HISTORICALLY SIGNIFICANT PLACES, EVENTS & THINGS TO DO
Art Galleries • Historical Sites • Lodging
Museums • Pueblos • Restaurants • Shopping
Spas • Touring the Countryside

Designed specifically for the traveler who wants
to get the most out of a short stay in town, with
suggestions chosen for variety and historical significance

Joel B. Stein
Photography by
Marcia Keegan

DESIGNED IN A WEB BOOK FORMAT™

INTERACTIVE WEB LINK PAGE
www.clearlightbooks.com/sfweek
See page viii for how to use this book.

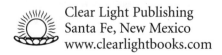

Clear Light Publishing
Santa Fe, New Mexico
www.clearlightbooks.com

To my dear wife, Mary, whose love of Santa Fe matches mine.

Text ©2003 Joel B. Stein
Photography ©2003 Marcia Keegan
Clear Light Publishing Corp.
823 Don Diego Avenue, Santa Fe, NM 87505
www.clearlightbooks.com

First Edition
10 9 8 7 6 5 4 3 2 1

Library of Congress Cataloging-in-Publication Data

Stein, Joel B.
  Santa Fe in a week : more or less / by Joel B. Stein ; photography by Marcia Keegan.— 1st ed.
      p. cm.
Includes index.
  ISBN 1-57416-072-9
1. Santa Fe (N.M.)—Guidebooks. 2. Santa Fe (N.M.)—Pictorial works.
3. Santa Fe (N.M.)—Tours. 4. Walking—New Mexico—Santa
Fe—Guidebooks. I. Keegan, Marcia. II. Title.
  F804.S23S74 2003
  917.89'560454—dc21
                                2003007206

Cover photograph ©Marcia Keegan
All photographs ©Marcia Keegan except as otherwise noted
Frontispiece map ©visitsantafe.com. Used with permission.
Ports of Call Books™ ©Clear Light Publishing Corp.
Web Book Format™ ©Clear Light Publishing Corp.
Cover design by Marcia Keegan and Carol O'Shea
Interior design and typography by Carol O'Shea
Printed in the U.S.A.

The information in this guidebook was confirmed at press time.
We recommend, however, that you call your destinations before travelling
to obtain the latest information.

WELCOMING MESSAGE
from Mayor Larry Delgado

We are happy to welcome you to a most unusual city, one settled by the Spanish long ago on land inhabited for centuries by the Pueblo Indians. Over the past 400 years, Santa Fe has been blended into a rich amalgam of tradition, ceremony, ritual and language, and as a result, it has become a different sort of place.

My Santa Fe family history goes back eleven generations; my wife's family, twelve generations. We've seen change—Santa Fe has grown and prospered over the years—but the sense of history, art and culture that has been part of our town for centuries remains constant and pure.

Your visit may be a short one, but our statistics tell us you'll be back to drink in the beauty of the land, meet our people, enjoy the scent of burning piñon on a winter's evening or wander through the many fascinating art galleries around town. We are pleased that you've chosen to visit Santa Fe—The City Different—and again, Bienvenido!

Saludos Amigos

Larry Delgado
Mayor of Santa Fe

TABLE OF CONTENTS

HOW TO USE THIS BOOK

WEB BOOK FORMAT™
An Interactive Reading Experience

The Web Book Format™ has been developed by Clear Light Publishing to enhance the reading experience with content and supplementary material accessible through the Internet. Each chapter in *Santa Fe in a Week or Less* is copiously referenced with Web sites that give you the ability to receive additional information and familiarize yourself with Santa Fe's many attractions. You can make reservations, explore museums and investigate side trips at your leisure, preparing yourself for the magic of Santa Fe in the Land of Enchantment.

The special feature of the Web Book Format™ is the Web link page on our Web site, www.clearlightbooks.com/sfweek, which lists the Web references in the book, making them easier to use. This free service for our readers and customers provides the availability of the latest information and updates, since Web sites and their addresses change frequently. To access the current links, simply go to our Web page and register your name and e-mail address. You will find all of our links and referenced sites searchable by category or site name. All you have to do is point and click.

The Web Book Format™ makes it easy and fun to explore the virtual Santa Fe. It can also assist you in planning your itinerary to maximize the enjoyment of your travel experience. You will feel as if you have been here before.

The authors and editors have made every effort to make sure that this guide is as accurate and up-to-date as possible. We realize, however, that many things can change after publication—some businesses close, new ones open, hours of operation and rates change, etc. We would love to hear from you about your experiences with this book, especially information that will help us keep the Web page up-to-date. Please e-mail your comments and suggestions to edit@clearlightbooks.com.

It is our hope and aspiration that we can enhance your travel experience and keep you coming back for years to enjoy every season in Santa Fe.

INTERACTIVE WEB LINK PAGE
www.clearlightbooks.com/sfweek

PREFACE

Bienvenido! Welcome to Santa Fe—the "City of Holy Faith." Whatever enticed you to come here, whoever told you of the wonderment you may experience here, we are delighted that you've arrived.

I've been a docent at the Palace of the Governors for several years, and, during that time, I have had the pleasure of connecting with people from all over the world! Most of these travelers say that they're visiting Santa Fe for less than a week, and many have come for only a day or so. Yet these visitors find themselves toting substantial stacks of guidebooks—formidable tomes dispensing far more information than the average person could possibly digest in such a brief time.

Taking a cue from you, our very welcome tourist, this book has been designed for the traveler who visits for a few days, a week or perhaps a touch more. We haven't noted every last thing there is to do or see in this magnificent, centuries-old city. That would be impossible and, in any event, contrary to our mission, which is to share with you several days worth of local Southwestern magic, history and highlights. Listed in the book are relevant, related Web sites, sites that will assist you in planning your trip and in making reservations.

To experience all of Santa Fe, you must come back and visit often! Or, perhaps you will decide to move here, as I did. Now, I'm happily immersed in this city of three cultures, living each day with history at every turn, charm on every city block—museums, music, theater, opera, hiking, skiing and, of course, fabulous dining. Who could ask for more?

Perhaps D.H. Lawrence said it best: "I think New Mexico was the greatest experience from the outside world that I have ever had. It certainly changed me forever.... The moment I saw the brilliant, proud morning sunshine high over the deserts of Santa Fe, something stood still in my soul, and I started to attend.... In the magnificent fierce morning of New Mexico one sprang awake, a new part of the soul woke up suddenly, and the world gave way to the new."

Enjoy,

Joel B. Stein

Santa Fe Time Line

1150–1400: Pueblo Indian villages are thriving along the Santa Fe River.

1598: Juan de Oñate claims New Mexico for Spain and establishes the first permanent European settlement in New Mexico (the second in the United States, following St. Augustine) near San Juan Pueblo, northwest of Santa Fe.

1609–10: Pedro de Peralta establishes the city of Santa Fe as Spain's northernmost administrative capital in the Southwest. The Palace of the Governors is built. El Camino Real becomes the supply route for the Spanish missions and colony, running from Mexico City to Santa Fe. Meanwhile, in 1607 the colony of Jamestown is founded in Virginia.

1680: The Pueblo Indians drive the Spanish out of New Mexico in the Pueblo Revolt. Meanwhile, European settlers are founding and settling new colonies on the East Coast.

1692: Diego de Vargas leads a Spanish military expedition back to Santa Fe and reclaims the area for the king of Spain.

1693–6: Diego de Vargas spends the next few years reconquering the outlying pueblos and bringing settlers.

1712: Santa Fe celebrates its first official Fiesta in thanksgiving for the reconquest. Meanwhile, the Eastern colonies are starting to yearn for independence. The buildup to the Revolutionary War and the war itself has little effect on Santa Fe, which still belongs to Mexico.

1792: Pedro Vial blazes a trail from Santa Fe to St. Louis and returns the following year, making the first complete journey over what will eventually be known as the Santa Fe Trail. Meanwhile, the U.S. Bill of Rights is now part of the Constitution.

1821: Mexico wins independence from Spain. Trader William Becknell arrives in Santa Fe to do business, opening up the Santa Fe Trail. Wagons roll into the Santa Fe Plaza, bringing millions of dollars of trade goods, new ideas and cultural influences.

1833: The first gold mines west of the Mississippi open in the Ortiz Mountains between Santa Fe and Albuquerque.

1834: New Mexico's first newspaper, *El Crepúsculo de la Libertad, The Dawn of Liberty*—is published in Santa Fe. Meanwhile, Texans are waging war for independence from Mexico.

1837: A group of northern New Mexican farmers and Indians band together to protest new taxes imposed by the Mexican government. Unrest follows.

1846: U.S. declares war on Mexico, and General Stephen W. Kearny occupies Santa Fe without firing a shot. The Territorial period begins.

1847: Territorial Governor Charles Bent is assassinated in Taos during a rebellion quickly quashed by U.S. forces.

1848: The Treaty of Guadalupe Hidalgo is signed. Mexico cedes New Mexico to the United States. Meanwhile, gold is discovered in California.

1850: New Mexico officially becomes a U.S. territory.

1851: Bishop Jean Baptiste Lamy founds the first English-language school in Santa Fe.

1861–2: Confederate soldiers from Texas invade New Mexico and occupy the Palace of the Governors. The Battle of Glorieta, just southeast of Santa Fe, ends Confederate control in New Mexico and squelches their plan to capture the West. The Civil War finally ends in 1865.

1869: Construction of the St. Francis Cathedral begins. Meanwhile, the transcontinental railroad is completed.

1879: Governor Lew Wallace writes a portion of *Ben Hur* in the Palace of the Governors. Meanwhile, Thomas Edison invents the lightbulb.

1880: The Atchison, Topeka and Santa Fe Railroad reaches Santa Fe via a spur line from the main station in Lamy. Travel along the Santa Fe Trail dies off.

1881: Santa Fe installs its first water and telegraph systems.

1892: New Mexico's new territorial Capitol building burns. Some suspect arson by those who wish Albuquerque to become the capital.

1907: The Palace of the Governors, scheduled for demolition, instead becomes a museum. Meanwhile, a few years earlier, 1903 saw the first World Series baseball game, the invention of the airplane, and the first movie, *The Great Train Robbery.*

1909: The joint Museum of New Mexico-School of American Archaeology, under the direction of Edgar Lee Hewitt, establishes the criteria for Santa Fe Style.

1912: New Mexico becomes the 47th state. The same year, the Titanic sinks in the North Atlantic.

1913: The Palace of the Governors is remodeled with a Pueblo Revival-style portal. Other buildings and new construction follow this trend.

1917: The New Mexico Museum of Fine Arts, also in Pueblo Revival style, is dedicated. Meanwhile, the United States enters World War I.

1922: The Southwestern Association for Indian Arts establishes the annual Indian Market, a show and sale that helps promote new and established Indian artists while bringing thousands of tourists to town every summer. Meanwhile, these years also see women get the right to vote, the first radio stations and the prohibition of the sale of alcoholic beverages.

1926: The Old Santa Fe Association is founded to help preserve the city's historical landmarks. Artist Will Shuster creates the giant puppet Zozobra, or Old Man Gloom. The burning of Zozobra quickly becomes a mainstay of the Santa Fe Fiesta.

1942: The federal government chooses the Los Alamos Boys School as the site for a secret project to develop an atomic bomb. Scientists and their families begin coming to the Santa Fe area. The U.S. is fighting in World War II.

1945: Scientists working in Los Alamos produce the world's first atomic bomb. The same year, the United States detonates two of these bombs in Japan, and World War II ends. The United Nations is set up to preserve peace and protect human rights.

1948: Indians receive the right to vote.

1957: Santa Fe adopts its Historic District Ordinance to help protect landmark buildings. John Crosby founds The Santa Fe Opera.

1961: Architect John Gaw Meem and other concerned residents establish the Historic Santa Fe Foundation to promote the preservation of the city's unique architectural character.

1966: New Mexico's present state Capitol, nicknamed the Roundhouse, is dedicated in Santa Fe. The Capitol is the only round Capitol and the only one without a dome in the country.

1980s: Celebrities "discover" Santa Fe and it becomes a trendy tourist destination as well as a popular spiritual center.

1987: The Santa Fe City Council adopts an archeological review ordinance protecting artifacts older than 75 years.

1997: The Georgia O'Keeffe Museum opens in July, 11 years after the death of the artist.

2002: The Spanish Colonial Arts Museum opens on Museum Hill.

2003 Momument to the European settlers of 1598 dedicated in Cathedral Park. Also dedicated is statue of the Blessed Kateri Tekakwitha (the first Native American saint) in front of St. Francis Cathedral.

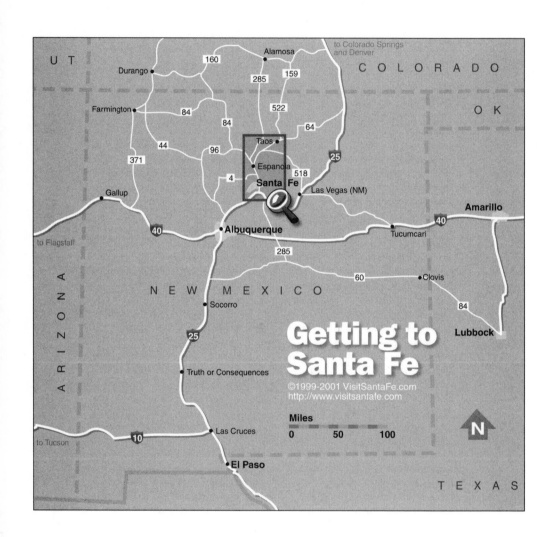

Getting to
Santa Fe

©1999-2001 VisitSantaFe.com
http://www.visitsantafe.com

TRAVEL INFORMATION

GENERAL INFORMATION REGARDING SANTA FE, ALBUQUERQUE AND TAOS

When going by air, most travelers fly into Albuquerque, then take the one-hour shuttle trip up to Santa Fe. A few airlines fly directly into Santa Fe, so we have included the information for that airport as well. Driving up to Taos from Santa Fe takes about an hour and a half.

Here are some links with useful information for Albuquerque, Santa Fe and Taos:

http://www.santafe.org/
(Santa Fe Convention and Visitors Bureau)
http://www.newmexico.org/
(New Mexico Department of Tourism, statewide attractions and maps)
http://nmculturenet.org/
(CultureNetWork, an on-line directory of artists, artisans, arts organizations, galleries and others involved in the cultural life of New Mexico)
http://www.collectorsguide.com/sf/sffa01.html
(introduction to Santa Fe)
http://www.santafe.com/
(Santa Fe On Line Magazine, listings and reviews of accommodations and restaurants with addresses and phone numbers, also attractions and the arts)
http://www.visitsantafe.com/
(listings and links for accommodations & restaurants, sorted by type, also activities, the arts and maps)
http://www.santafeinformation.com/
(similar to other general information sites above, but includes a Web cam)
http://www.thesantafesite.com/index.html
(listings and some links for accommodations and restaurants, events and outdoor activities, also some features relating to Santa Fe subjects)

Left: Santa Fe is located in the north central part of New Mexico. Map ©visitsantafe.com. Used with permission.

http://www.sfaol.com/
(similar to above sites, contains a wider variety of links)
http://sfweb.ci.santa-fe.nm.us/
(official Web site of the city of Santa Fe)
http://www.santafechamber.com/
(Santa Fe Chamber of Commerce)
http://www.santafean.com/
(Web site for the Santa Fean *magazine, contains features relating specifically to Santa Fe, especially art and culture, also selected local links)*
http://www.nmmagazine.com/
*(*New Mexico Magazine, *statewide attractions and features, also Internet links sorted by category, including over 1,000 for Santa Fe alone)*
http://www.abqcvb.org/
(Albuquerque Convention & Visitors Bureau)
http://www.gacc.org/
(The Greater Albuquerque Chamber of Commerce)
http://www.collectorsguide.com/ab/abfa01.html
(introduction to Albuquerque)
http://www.taoschamber.com/index.php3
(Taos Chamber of Commerce)
http://www.skinewmexico.com/
(Ski New Mexico)

AIRLINE INFORMATION

All major U.S. airlines fly into the Albuquerque International Sunport. You can rent a car at the Sunport, or, you may take a shuttle to Santa Fe (advance reservations are recommended). The distance to Santa Fe from Albuquerque is about 62 miles, and the drive takes about an hour. Here are some numbers you may wish to keep on hand:

Airline Reservations & Flight Information
(505) 244-7733 (or call individual airline)
You can get detailed flight information from your airline's Web site or from the following:
http://www.cabq.gov/airport/
(Albuquerque International Sunport)

Airport Police Office
(505) 244-7700
Lost and Found/Paging/Skycap Assistance/Airport Parking Information
(or call individual airline)

SHUTTLES TO AND FROM SANTA FE

Santa Fe Shuttle
(888) 833-2300 or (505) 243-2300
http://www.shuttlesantafe.com/
(Santa Fe Shuttle)

Twin Hearts Express
(800) 654-9456 or (505) 751-1201
http://www.twinheartsexpress.com/
(Twin Hearts Express)

Sandia Shuttle Express
(888) 775-5696 or (505) 474-5696
http://www.sandiashuttle.com/
(Sandia Shuttle Express)

Eldorado Hotel Shuttle Schedule
http://www.eldoradohotel.com/shuttle.html
(Eldorado Hotel Shuttle Schedule)

SANTA FE MUNICIPAL AIRPORT

Santa Fe's municipal airport is located at the southwest corner of the city and handles all types of private aircraft. United Express provides commuter service into and out of Santa Fe.

Santa Fe Municipal Airport
Airport Information Line
(505) 955-2908
http://www.airnav.com/airport/SAF
(Santa Fe Municipal Airport)
http://www.nmohwy.com/s/saf.htm
(on line Highways – Santa Fe Municipal Airport)

United Express
(800) 241-6522 or (505) 473-4118
http://www.skywest.com
(United Express, operated by Skywest)
http://www.ual.com
(United Airlines, parent company of Skywest)

Clouds like these could bring rain almost any day during the summer.

Santa Fe Jet Center (FBO)
(505) 471-2525
http://www.santafejet.biz/
(Santa Fe Jet Center)

Santa Fe Executive Aviation (FBO)
(505) 471-2700
http://www.santafeexecutive.com/
(Santa Fe Executive Aviation)

AMTRAK

Albuquerque and Santa Fe (Lamy station) are served by Amtrak. Amtrak's Southwest Chief trains—eastbound from Los Angeles and westbound from Chicago—meet each afternoon at Lamy, New Mexico.

Call the Lamy Shuttle at (505) 982-8829 to arrange transportation to Santa Fe (14 miles, about 15 minutes' drive time), or, notify your hotel for pickup.

Amtrak Information and Reservations
Local station in Lamy: (505) 466-4511
nationwide reservations: (800) 872-7245
http://www.amtrak.com/
(Amtrak Rail Service)

SANTA FE'S WEATHER & WHAT TO WEAR

At 7,000 feet above sea level, Santa Fe is a high desert country dotted with piñon and ponderosa pines as opposed to the giant saguaro and other cacti of lower desert elevations. We're close to the clouds and close to the sun, and our 300 days of sunshine per year are accompanied by very low humidity. This makes for warm days (rarely more than the mid-90s during June, July and August) and cool, "good sleeping" nights.

Dress in Santa Fe is casual, and shorts are fine for most summer days. The temperature drops soon after sunset, so bring a sweater or jacket along with you. Should you attend the beautiful Santa Fe Opera or other outdoor evening event, you may need a blanket or warm jacket. (We once sat next to a couple from Phoenix wearing short-sleeved shirts and wound up sharing our blanket with them.) Rainshowers are short but sudden, and it is wise to check the local forecast before attending outdoor concerts.

The dress code here is relaxed, so leave your tie at home. Many locals wear a Santa Fe tuxedo when they go out on the town. What is a Santa Fe tuxedo, you ask? Well, it consists of a cowboy shirt with a bolo instead of a tie, jeans, a handcrafted leather belt with a silver buckle, cowboy boots, a cowboy hat and a sport jacket. And that's really dressing up!

Warmth often lingers into early November. After that, layer your clothes; even in winter the daytime temperatures are much warmer than those after sundown. A warm ski jacket is perfect for snowy days. We have 40-degree swings in temperature within a 24-hour period. In the winter, you may wake up to 15-degree mornings, and by 1:00 in the afternoon the temperature could be up around 55 degrees!

Average Weather Statistics

Average Temperature	January	High 42–Low 19
	July	High 86–Low 57
Average Rainfall	12–14 inches	
Average Snowfall	17.5 inches	

For more information, check out the The Weather Channel's Web page for Santa Fe:

http://www.weather.com/weather/local/USNM0292?x=12&whatprefs=&y=13

(The Weather Channel--search for Santa Fe, NM.)

The state flag displays the Zia sun symbol.

STATE SYMBOLS & A BIT OF TRIVIA

The State Flag of New Mexico

New Mexico's current flag is one of many to have flown over the state. It was preceded by the flags of Spain, Mexico, the Confederate States of America, the United States and an earlier state flag. That first state flag featured a small American flag in the upper left quadrant, a state seal in the lower right and the words "New Mexico" stitched diagonally in red across a dark blue background. This flag flew from 1912 to 1925, when it was replaced by the current flag, which features the red sun symbol called a "Zia" (the sun symbol of the Zia Pueblo Indians) on a field of gold. Red and gold were the colors of Queen Isabella de Castile and represented the colors of old Spain.

http://www.50states.com/flag/nmflag.htm
(New Mexico state flag)
http://www.worldatlas.com/Webimage/flags/usa/nmflag.htm
(New Mexico state flag)

The Zia Sun Symbol

New Mexico's distinctive Zia sun symbol is closely associated with the state, whose motto is the Land of Enchantment. Inspired by a design found on a 19th-century water jar from Zia Pueblo, the symbol is made up of a circular sun with linear rays extending in four directions. To the Zia people, four is a significant number. It incorporates the four directions of the Earth and the four seasons of the year, along with the four times of the day—sunrise, noon, evening and night. It also represents life's four divisions—childhood, youth, adulthood and old age. The symbol states that everything is bound together in a circle of life, without beginning and without end. The Zia believe that in this Great Brotherhood of all things, man has four sacred obligations to maintain—a strong body, a clear mind, a pure spirit and a devotion to the welfare of his people.

http://www.newmexiconet.com/nm_photos_zia_symbol_00.htm
(Zia symbol explanation)
http://www.nmsu.edu/~bho/zia.html
(Zia Sun Symbol meaning)

Other Official State Symbols

State Amphibian

The 2003 state Legislature chose the **New Mexico spadefoot toad** (*Spea multiplicata*) as the official state amphibian. This medium-sized desert-dwelling toad is greenish, gray or brown, with scattered darker spots or blotches. Its eyes show vertical pupils in bright light. Each hind foot features a wedge-shaped spade, which enables it to burrow deep into the ground. These toads are most easily seen and heard after a summer rain. They are found statewide.

http://www.fw.vt.edu/fishex/nmex_main/species/020080.htm
(general information)
http://www.sonoran-herpetology.com/azsonsin/Spea_multiplicata_pics.html
(pictures of spadefoot toad)
http://coloherp.org/geo/species/spespmu.php
(from guide to reptiles and amphibians of Colorado)
http://www.tpwd.state.tx.us/nature/education/tracker/amphibians/species5.htm
(to hear its call)

State Animal

The **black bear** *(Ursus americanus)* is common in wooded areas throughout New Mexico. Smokey, probably the most famous bear in the history of the United States, was a New Mexico cub found cowering in a tree after a forest fire in the Lincoln National Forest near Capitan, New Mexico.

http://www.enchantedlearning.com/subjects/mammals/bear/Amblackcoloring.shtml
(black bears)
http://www.smokeybear.com/vault/default.asp
(Smokey the Bear)

State Bird

The friendly **roadrunner** *(Geococcyx californianus)*, a type of cuckoo, can run at speeds of up to 20 mph! Adult birds are as large as two feet long, half of that being tail. The birds rarely fly and do not migrate.

http://www.enchantedlearning.com/subjects/birds/printouts/Roadrunner.shtml
(roadrunners)
http://www.50states.com/bird/roadrunn.htm
(roadrunners)
http://www.desertusa.com/mag98/sep/papr/road.html
(detailed information)
http://www.passporttotexas.com/birds/jul00.html
(detailed information including its call)

State Butterfly

The **Sandia hairstreak** (*Callophrys [Sandia] mcfarlandi*), a small green-and-gold butterfly found in much of the state, was chosen the state butterfly in 2003.

http://www.npwrc.usgs.gov/resource/distr/lepid/bflyusa/NM/306.htm
(general information)
http://www.nearctica.com/butter/plate8/Cmcfar.htm
(general information)

State Cookie

In 1989 the **bizcochito** *(bees-ko-CHEE-toh)* was named the state cookie. New Mexico is the first state to have an official state cookie and probably the only one to use the traditional lard instead of butter as a chief cookie ingredient.

http://www.hungrybrowser.com/phaedrus/m121201.htm#1
(bizcochito recipe)
http://www.statehousegirls.net/nm/symbols/cookie/
(recipe and information)

A family enjoying a typical Santa Fe pastime,
going after the state fish in the Rió Grande.

State Fish

The **Rio Grande cutthroat trout** *(Onchorhynchus clarki virginalis)* is native to the mountain streams and lakes of Northern New Mexico.

http://www.nmwild.org/wild/fa_trout.htm

(Rio Grande cutthroat trout information)

http://sangres.com/sports/fish/fishingnm.htm

(New Mexico fishing rules and regulations)

State Flower

The **yucca** *(Yucca glauca)*, called "Our Lord's Candles" by early settlers who admired the beautiful flowers of this cactus, is abundant throughout New Mexico.

http://www.visitsantafe.com/navigate.cfm?nav=showphoto.cfm_photoID=347

(yucca photo)

http://www.geobop.com/World/NA/US/NM/Flower.htm

(general information)

A Zuni Pueblo woman wearing needlepoint turquoise jewelry,
a typical Zuni design. The large hand-painted pot on her head is called an olla.

State Fossil

The **Coelophysis** (SEE-low-FIE-sis), an ancient, meat-eating creature, is
New Mexico's only Triassic-era dinosaur. Originally discovered in Rio
Arriba County, this dinosaur was deemed the state fossil in 1987.
Coelophysis (which means "hollow form") was a small, lightweight
dinosaur that walked on two long legs and had light, hollow bones.

http://www.enchantedlearning.com/subjects/dinosaurs/dinos/Coelophysis.shtml
(Coelophysis)

State Gem

Turquoise *(hydrated copper aluminum phosphate)*, a gemstone favored
by the Indians long before the Spanish arrived, is the most popular gem
of jewelers and silversmiths in New Mexico.

http://jewelry.about.com/library/weekly/aa062902a.htm
(about turquoise and how to buy it)

http://www.americana.net/tourq.html
(history of turquoise)

http://www.americana.net/jewelry.html
(history of American Indian jewelry)
http://www.thesantafesite.com/Articles/truthonturquoise.html
(information on buying turquoise)

State Grass

The **blue gramma** *(Bouteloua gracilis)* is found all over the state, especially on grasslands and bottomlands between altitudes of 3,000 and 8,000 feet. It thrives in dry climates.

http://www.turf.uiuc.edu/turfSpecies/Boutelouagracilis.html
(information)
http://twofrog.com/blgram.html
(photo of blue gramma grass)

State Insect

The **tarantula hawk wasp** *(Pepsis formosa)* was selected as the state insect by elementary-school vote in 1989. It is found in New Mexico and other Southwestern states.

http://www.desertusa.com/mag01/sep/papr/thawk.html
(tarantula hawk wasp)
http://www.geobop.com/World/NA/US/NM/Insect.htm
(general information)
http://homeschooling.about.com/library/blnmbug.htm
(general information)

State Reptile

The **New Mexico whiptail lizard** became the official state reptile in 2003. All these little striped lizards are female—they actually reproduce by cloning themselves!

http://animal.discovery.com/convergence/lizards/dads/dads.html
(lizards without dads)

State Slogan

Adopted by the Legislature in 1975, "Everybody is somebody in New Mexico" is the official state slogan for business, commerce and industry in New Mexico.

A waitress at Rancho de Chimayó holds a typical Northern New Mexico dinner entrée, featuring chile-smothered enchiladas with a side of frijoles.

State Tree

The **piñon pine** *(Pinus edulis)*, a sturdy, slow-growing little evergreen, flourishes over vast areas of the state. The piñon produces tiny, tasty nuts that are highly prized by gourmet cooks, and the pleasant, distinctive scent of burning logs perfumes New Mexico's air in cold weather.

http://www.botanik.uni-bonn.de/conifers/pi/pin/edulis.htm

(general information)

http://homeschooling.about.com/library/blnmtree.htm
(general information)
http://www.na.fs.fed.us/spfo/pubs/silvics_manual/Volume_1/pinus/edulis.htm
(very detailed information)
http://medplant.nmsu.edu/pinon.htm
(pictures and medicinal uses)
http://www.yvwiiusdinvnohii.net/NAIFood/NAIrecipes3.htm
(North American Indian recipes with piñon nuts)
http://www.globalgourmet.com/food/egg/egg0597/pinon.html
(Piñon Cornbread from Mark Miller's Coyote Café in Santa Fe)

State Vegetables

Chiles and *frijoles!* **Chile,** often teamed up with **pinto beans,** is a unique
element of the New Mexico diet. Chile plants were brought by the
Spanish settlers to New Mexico from Mexico, where the Aztecs had cul-
tivated the plants for centuries. Chile is the New Mexico state vegetable
even though it is technically a fruit.

http://www.nmsu.edu/~ucomm/Panorama/fall2002/center.html
(all about chile)
http://americancookbooks.com/american_gazette_the_history_of.htm
(history of chile)
http://www.newmexico.org/culture
(Jemez Pueblo chile images)
http://www-psych.nmsu.edu/~linda/chile.htm
(chile recipes and links)

Pinto beans have been a staple of the Pueblo Indians' diet since prehis-
toric times. An excellent source of protein, the medium-sized pinto
bean (*frijole*) is a hybrid that takes its name from the Spanish word for
"painted." Light brown, with dark-brown spatter markings, pintos fade
to a uniform dull brown color after cooking.

http://www.mothering.com/recipes/pinto-beans.shtml
(recipe for pinto beans)
http://co.essortment.com/drypintobeans_rjtr.htm
(everything about cooking pinto beans)

For more information on state symbols:
http://www.netstate.com/states/symb/nm_symb.htm
(state symbols with links and year adopted)

After moaning for several long minutes, Zozobra finally bursts into flames.

ZOZOBRA

Santa Fe artist Will Shuster (1893–1969) drew heavily upon local customs and ceremonies as subjects for his art, so it seems only fitting that he played a part in creating one of Santa Fe's most popular rituals. Perhaps the most well-loved and well-known Shuster creation is Zozobra, the twenty-foot paper puppet, also known as Old Man Gloom, whose annual burning signifies the exoneration of last year's sorrows and the beginning of the Santa Fe Fiesta. Originally created by Shuster in 1926, Zozobra has become a Santa Fe legend (see also page 196).

http://www.zozobra.com
(Zozobra in pictures and information about current year's burning)
http://www.zozobra.com/ zhistory.html
(history of Zozobra)

FOR TRIVIA BUFFS

Santa Fe is not named for a saint, but you're in the right "realm." The name "Santa Fe" is Spanish and means "Holy Faith." It was settled by the Spanish in 1609. Don Pedro de Peralta of Spain made Santa Fe the administrative capital of the area. It is the oldest capital in the United States. In the early days, the town was known as La Villa Real de la Santa Fe de San Francisco de Asis, "The Royal City of Santa Fe of St. Francis of Assisi." Don Pedro de Peralta became the third of sixty governors of this Spanish colony.

http://www.santafe.org/Visiting_Santa_Fe/History/
(Santa Fe history)

General Lew Wallace, a New Mexico territorial governor in 1879, wrote part of his novel, *Ben Hur*, while residing in the Palace of the Governors in Santa Fe. The museum still has the chair he sat upon while writing. First published in 1880, this book was made into a movie in 1959 starring Charlton Heston.

http://www.ben-hur.com/index2.html
(Ben Hur Museum)
http://www.wvu.edu/~lawfac/jelkins/lp-2001/wallace_lew.html
(Lew Wallace)

The province that was once Spanish New Mexico included all of present-day New Mexico, most of Colorado and Arizona, and slices of Utah, Texas, Oklahoma, Kansas and Wyoming. The original American territory of New Mexico created by Congress in 1850 included all of New Mexico and Arizona plus parts of Colorado, Nevada, and Utah. The boundaries of present-day New Mexico were drawn by Congress in 1863, but New Mexico didn't become the 47th state until January 6, 1912.

http://www.50states.com/facts/newmex.htm
(New Mexico facts)

Classified climatically as a high desert, Santa Fe is 7,000 feet above sea level and averages about 300 days of sunshine a year. New Mexico's 10,000-foot topographical relief—from 2,840 to 13,160 feet—includes six of the world's seven life zones. It comprises 122,666 square miles and is the fifth-largest state in the country.

http://sfweb.ci.santa-fe.nm.us/sfpl/nmlink.html
(Santa Fe Public Library)

Santa Fe is and was the home of many celebrities such as novelists Willa Cather, Tony Hillerman and D.H. Lawrence; artists Georgia O'Keeffe, Allan Houser, Gustave Baumann and R.C. Gorman; actors Greer Garson, Errol Flynn, Gene Hackman, Val Kilmer, Carole Burnett, Shirley MacLaine, Ali MacGraw, and singers John Denver and Burl Ives.

http://www.newmexico.org/Fun/famous.html
(list of famous New Mexicans)

Santa Fe has also been home to the notorious, including the famous outlaw Billy the Kid. It is even rumored that he washed dishes and played the piano at La Fonda (the Exchange Hotel at that time), but he didn't even know how to play the piano!

http://www.angelfire.com/mi2/billythekid/index.html
(Billy the Kid)

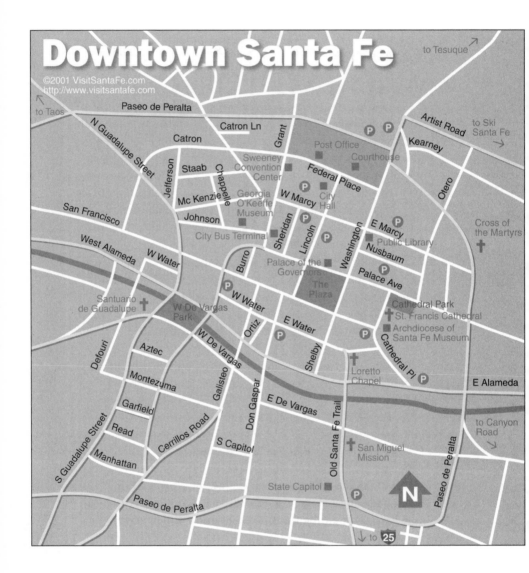

THE DOWNTOWN WALKING TOUR OF OLD SANTA FE

Many old buildings in downtown Santa Fe have significant historical importance. In recognition of this, they are listed in the Historic Santa Fe Registry. While walking about town, you will see plaques on the outside walls of those designated as historic sites worthy of preservation.

http://www.historicsantafe.com/Registry.htm

(registry of Santa Fe historic places)

BEGIN AT THE PLAZA

The Plaza: The Center of Social Life

The Plaza site was laid out by decree from King Philip II of Spain, a decree that applied to the construction of any town in the New World. King Philip II desired that all towns grow out symmetrically from a central gathering place.

Called La Plaza de Armas in the 17th century, the Plaza hosted military parades and religious festivals and eventually became the center of commerce and social life in Santa Fe. In the beginning, it was surrounded by a wall to keep enemies out, and at one time it housed a bullring. During the 19th century, a decorative gazebo featured band concerts. The trail route of the Camino Real, upon which wagons carried supplies from Mexico City (1598–1821), and the Santa Fe Trail (1821–1880) ended at the Plaza, where wares were unloaded and sold.

The obelisk in the center of the Plaza is a monument erected in 1868 to commemorate local soldiers, including the heroes of the Civil War from the battles of Valverde, Glorieta, Cañon de Apache, Pigeon's

Left: Map of Santa Fe with some of the main destinations marked. Map ©visitsantafe.com. Used with permission.

Local celebrations and parades frequently take place in front of
the Palace of the Governors.

Ranch and Peralta. These 1862 battles were against the Confederate
armies that briefly occupied Santa Fe and Albuquerque while on their
way to attempt to reach the Colorado gold fields. The Confederates had
hoped to use the gold to help subsidize their war effort and, possibly, to
open a seaport in San Francisco. They never made it to their destination,
and this was one important turning point of the war (see also page 137).
The obelisk also honors men who died in campaigns against Indians.

Directly across from the Palace of the Governors sat a beautifully
decorated adobe military chapel, La Castrense, once used by the soldiers but no longer there. The only remaining chapel artifact is a stone
altar screen preserved at the Cristo Rey Church where Canyon Road
meets Camino Cabra. Its centerpiece is Santiago or St. James, the
patron saint of Spain.

In the 1600s most of the buildings surrounding the Plaza were military ones. During the 1800s shops began to appear. From 1860 to the
late 1800s Jewish merchants who had immigrated from Germany
opened retail businesses all around the Plaza. Most of these buildings
were Victorian in architecture.

http://www.santafenow.com/links/april99/
(history of Santa Fe Plaza)

The Palace of the Governors:
The History Museum of New Mexico

The Palace of the Governors, most likely begun in 1609, is the oldest continuously occupied government building in the United States. Designed by the Spanish conquistadors under the direction of Governor Pedro de Peralta, it was one of several government buildings, or *casas reales*. It later became known as the Palace of the Governors.

The building was constructed with adobe bricks—compositions made of mud, sand, water, straw and sometimes dried manure. Adobe hardens to a very tough consistency and lasts a long time; some of the original adobe walls are still visible inside the building.

Adobe bricks probably originated in the Middle East. The use of adobe spread to Spain, when the African Moors occupied that country for many centuries.

The Spanish conquistadors brought the adobe brick construction method to Santa Fe, where it was perfectly suited to the high-desert climate and the clay soils. The Pueblo Indians had been building their dwellings for many years with adobe, but not in brick form. Instead, they added successive layers of wet clay to the tops of walls, letting the clay dry, then adding more. This was known as puddle adobe. So the Spanish taught the Indians the adobe brick method and in return the Indians passed on their roof building method to the Spanish. This consisted of using *vigas* or tree trunks to hold up the roof and *latillas* or small twigs between the vigas to keep the roof itself (dirt) from falling into the rooms.

The Palace of the Governors has had many incarnations. Beginning as a fort, it was also a home to farmers, traders, missionaries and soldiers. The Supreme Court met in the Chapel; Territorial governors lived in the building prior to the adoption of statehood in 1912; and the Territorial Legislature met inside its walls. At one time, part of the building was a post office and part of it was a prison. In fact, in 1807, Lt. Zebulon Pike (of Pike's Peak fame) was incarcerated there by the Spaniards.

The grounds housed much livestock, various stables, numerous gardens and a spring offering a natural water supply. It is thought that, early on, the grounds extended several blocks to the north.

In 1909, Jesse Nusbaum, a photographer and archaeologist, was given the huge undertaking of turning the Palace of the Governors into the New Mexico History Museum, which he completed by 1912. He is credited with restoring the Pueblo look to the Palace—what he called Pueblo Revival and we know today as "Santa Fe Style"—a look that became the predominant format for most local buildings.

http://palaceofthegovernors.org/

(Palace of the Governors site)

EAST PALACE AVENUE & DOWNTOWN

The art gallery on the corner of East Palace and Washington Avenues was a gasoline station in the days-of-old (pre-1937) Route 66. Cars used the portal in front to pull in and "fill 'er up."

Trujillo Plaza
109 East Palace Avenue

This building and courtyard was the office of the Atomic Energy Commission, where scientists were processed for the highly secret Manhattan Project. They were then transported to Los Alamos, where their mailing address was Box 1663, Santa Fe, New Mexico. Children born in Los Alamos at that time have Box 1663 on their birth certificate as their place of birth. In today's world this is a badge of some distinction.

When they arrived in Santa Fe, the scientists' wives were not enamored of the town, which in the early forties had almost no restaurants, close to nothing in the way of shopping opportunities and only one movie theater, the Lensic. Little did they realize that Los Alamos had far fewer amenities!

Prince Plaza
113½ East Palace Avenue

Originally, the small courtyard that now houses The Shed restaurant (see page 83) was the 19th-century home of a French Canadian trader, Antoine Roubidoux. In 1879, Bradford Prince, a Territorial Governor and Supreme Court Justice, moved in and lived there until 1919.

Sena Plaza
125 East Palace Avenue

This romantic hacienda and courtyard was once home to the Sena family of Santa Fe. The complex, nearly 200 years old now, was originally purchased by Juan Sena. He and his wife had 21 children, so, clearly, the hacienda began to grow. His son, José, eventually enlarged it to 33

East Palace Avenue.

rooms, including a second-story ballroom! When the Territorial Capitol burned down in 1892, the Legislature temporarily convened here (See also page 77).

http://www.visitsantafe.com/businesspage.cfm?businessid=1947
(Sena Plaza)
http://www.visitsantafe.com/businesspage.cfm?BusinessID=1281
(La Casa Sena restaurant)

Cathedral Park

Crossing over East Palace onto Cathedral Place, we pass some pillars and a gate that used to be the entry to the old St. Vincent Sanatorium, built in 1911 to care for victims of tuberculosis. The land around that entry is now called Cathedral Park.

In the middle of the Park is the Cuarto Centenario Monu-ment, built in memory of the first Spanish colonists, friars and soldiers who came to the area in 1598. Erected in 2003, the monument depicts tools used at that time as well as the animals that were part of people's lives so long ago.

St. Francis Cathedral
213 Cathedral Place

Before the cathedral was built, several adobe churches stood in that same spot. The first church was destroyed during the 1680 Pueblo Revolt and was replaced by La Parroquia (parish church), built between 1714 and 1717.

When the first archbishop of Santa Fe arrived, he was not enamored of the brown stucco look of the building. He was determined to build a new and vibrant church in the French Romanesque style that he felt was closer to his idea of a proper cathedral. Archbishop Jean Bapiste Lamy and architects from his native France designed the cathedral; the cornerstone was laid in 1869 and the building completed in 1886. Note that the steeples normally seen on cathedrals aren't present: the archbishop ran out of funds. Recently, when a group volunteered money to build steeples, the parishoners rejected the idea. They like it the way it is.

The bishop brought over Italian stonecutters to quarry blocks of yellow limestone from a site miles from Santa Fe. That sleepy little town, now named Lamy, is the main local Amtrak train stop (see page 55).

The cathedral was built around the old Parroquia, and after the walls were up, the old church was demolished and the adobe blocks used as landfill in front of the new church. However, the bishop did preserve a section of the old church that today houses *La Conquistadora*—also known *Nuestra Señora de la Paz* (*Our Lady of Peace*)—a small willow statue that is considered to be the oldest Madonna in the United States.

http://www.dreamwater.com/blueelf/lady.htm
(theft of La Conquistadora)
http://www.evanderputten.org/special/newmexico/sfcathedral.htm
(St. Francis Cathedral)

La Fonda
100 East San Francisco Street

Directly across from the cathedral sits La Fonda, Santa Fe's oldest hotel. Its story parallels much of Santa Fe's history. It began in 1600 as a *fonda*, or inn, when an Alarid family home was turned into a place for traders to stay. It then became the United States Hotel (1846-48), and afterwards, until 1919, the Exchange Hotel.

The present day La Fonda (The Inn) was built in the 1920s on the site of the former hotel. Mary Jane Colter, an architect and decorator

St. Francis Cathedral.

who devised El Tovar and the Phantom Ranch in the Grand Canyon, designed the interior, including the furniture and the lamps. The hotel was owned and operated by Fred Harvey, who was renowned throughout the West as a concessionaire and as the creator of the Harvey Girls concept of courteous, intelligent and impeccably neat waitresses.

http://www.kaibab.org/gc/images/mjcolter.htm
(Mary Jane Colter)

http://jeff.scott.tripod.com/mjcolter.html
(Mary Jane Colter, Arizona Women Hall of Fame)

Many famous people signed La Fonda's guest register, among them Colonel John Fremont, General and Mrs. Ulysses S. Grant and President and Mrs. Rutherford B. Hayes. More modern well-known guests included Lily Pons, Salvador Dali, Elliott Roosevelt and Lord and Lady Halifax.

http://saints.css.edu/mkelsey/gppg.html
(Ulysses S. Grant Network)

In 1968, Sam Ballen bought the hotel and has continued to upgrade and modernize it while preserving its traditional Southwestern look (see also pages 78 and 99).

http://www.lafondasantafe.com/
(La Fonda)

Water Street

After you pass the cathedral, turn west onto Water Street and look behind you. You'll glimpse a portion of Archbishop Lamy's garden, a horticultural delight far more extensive in his day. The archbishop was an avid gardener and exchanged much gardening information with Flora Spiegelberg, wife of one of the German Jewish merchants in town. Because she spoke Latin, he asked her to teach catechism to his young Catholic parishioners, and she agreed to do so. Those interactions were but one fine example of people needing each other and working together in the frontier town of Santa Fe.

http://www.sfaol.com/history/bishop.html
(Archbishop Lamy's garden)
http://elibrary.unm.edu/oanm/NmU/nmu1%23mss18sc/nmu1%23mss18sc_m4.html
(Flora Spiegelberg biography)

Water Street was so named because of the occasional overflow onto that street from the Santa Fe River. It is said that raw sewage sometimes ran down the street, then named the Rio Chiquito (1880s), and that this disastrous occurrence continued occasionally into the 1920s. It was hardly the charming place to walk that it is today.

We continue walking down Water Street, turning south onto Old Santa Fe Trail, the route taken into town by the wagon trains traveling from Missouri.

Loretto Chapel
207 Old Santa Fe Trail

Our Lady of Light (Loretto) Chapel was built between 1873 and 1878 by the same Italian stonecutters who built St. Francis Cathedral. Modeled after the Sainte-Chapelle Church in Paris, it is a small, lovely chapel now privately owned and frequently used for weddings and concerts. The land next to it, currently occupied by the Inn at Loretto, was until 1968 home to the Loretto Academy for Girls. A statue of Our Lady of Lourdes stands atop the chapel.

The chapel gained fame for the spiral staircase built within and the mysterious, mystical story about the workman who constructed it. Originally, the chapel had no staircase to the choir loft. A staircase was needed, and the nuns made countless novenas to St. Joseph asking for his help. As the story goes, a carpenter arrived one day and agreed to assist. He fashioned an amazing circular staircase with two 360-degree turns and no center support, and then left without being paid. The

The famous spiral staircase at Loretto Chapel, a favorite site for weddings.

nuns thought that the carpenter was in fact St. Joseph. Present-day historians attribute the work to Francois-Jean Rochas of Vif, Isere, France, but the legend of St. Joseph still captures the imagination. The mystery of the staircase has been the subject of television programs, including *Unsolved Mysteries*, and a dramatic presentation on the subject.

http://www.lorettochapel.com/

(Loretto Chapel)

http://www.evanderputten.org/special/newmexico/loretto.htm

(Loretto Chapel)

Walking along the Old Santa Fe Trail (1821–1880) we pass the Inn at Loretto, built in 1975 in the Pueblo style. Look down at the Santa Fe River while crossing West Alameda Street. It's a dry river most of the year, except during spring runoff.

http://www.americanrivers.org/tableofcontents/santafe.htm

(Santa Fe River)

http://www.hotelloretto.com/

(Inn at Loretto)

OLD EAST DE VARGAS STREET AREA

Barrio de Analco

East De Vargas Street marks the beginning of the Barrio de Analco, or "district on the other side of the river." Next to the Plaza, this is the oldest settlement of European origin. It was actually constructed by Tlaxcalan Indians brought from Mexico as servants by the Spanish and the Franciscan Missionaries.

http://www.nmhu.edu/research/sftrail/barrio.htm
(Barrio de Analco)

San Miguel Mission
401 Old Santa Fe Trail

The San Miguel Mission, built around 1610, was perhaps the first church in the United States, thus it is also known as the "Oldest Church." During the Pueblo Revolt of 1680 (the only successful revolt of its kind in the United States), the Indians burned the roof of the church.

After the Spanish regained control of Santa Fe in 1693, they set about restoring the mission, work that was completed around 1710. This time it became a fortress, with new outer walls and added battlements to the roof. No further battles occurred, and by the 1800s the church had again been altered to include a triple-tiered tower. It was changed one more time, in 1870, to its current square tower configuration.

In 1798, an altar screen was added to include the impressive guilded statue of St. Michael, the patron saint of the Franciscan brothers. It was brought from Mexico in 1709 and was carried around New Mexico to help raise money for the rebuilding of the church.

http://www.nmhu.edu/research/sftrail/miguel.htm
(San Miguel Mission)
http://www.nmculture.org/cgi-bin/instview.cgi?_recordnum=SM
(San Miguel Mission)
http://www.evanderputten.org/special/newmexico/sanmiguel.htm
(Chapel of San Miguel)

Oldest House in Santa Fe
215 East De Vargas Street

Based on Adolph Bandelier's study that the foundation of this house dates back to a pueblo (circa A.D. 1250) and the *vigas* reveal their age as

San Miguel Mission, perhaps the oldest church in the U.S..

coming from the 1740 to 1767 time frame, this would support the house's claim to being the oldest house in town. Some believe this is actually the oldest standing house in the U.S.A. Whether or not this is true, it certainly is one of the oldest. The interior is a stunning example of Spanish colonial times, with its remaining dirt floor, corner fireplace, and traditional *viga* and *latilla* ceiling. A restaurant, Upper Crust Pizza (see page 84) now uses it as its rear dining room.

http://www.tedmontgomery.com/santafe/#top
(oldest church and oldest house)
http://www.planetware.com/photos/US/NMSFODHS.HTM
(photo of oldest house)

Santa Fe Playhouse
142 East De Vargas Street

The oldest theater west of the Mississippi, this unique playhouse was incorporated in 1922 by well-known writer Mary Austin. In 1962 it moved into its present home, an adobe building with a late-1800s life as a livery stable followed by tenure as a blacksmith shop (see also page 50).

http://www.santafeplayhouse.org/
(Santa Fe Playhouse)

The Roque Tudesqui House
129–135 East De Vargas Street

The west section of this house was sold to Italian-born Roque Tudesqui, a Santa Fe Trail trader, sometime before 1841. The Territorial-style house has three-foot-thick adobe walls and an outrageously beautiful 75-year-old wisteria vine that uses an adjacent tree to weave its way to the sky.

http://www.historicsantafe.com/Tudesqui.htm

(Roqui Tudesqui House)

The Gregorio Crespin House
132 East De Vargas Street

This homestead, built between 1720 and 1747, was part of the property owned by Gregorio Crespin and then sold to Bartolome Marquez for 50 pesos. The original land grant was given by General Vargas to Juan de Leon Brito, a Mexican Tlaxcalan Indian who, from 1692 to 1693, helped the Spanish reclaim Santa Fe from the Pueblo Indians.

http://www.nmhu.edu/research/sftrail/barrio.htm

(Barrio de Analco Historic District)

At the end of the Barrio de Analco, you can catch a glimpse of the state Capitol building (built 1964–65). It is called the "Roundhouse," as it resembles an Indian kiva in its round shape. From the air, the New Mexican sun symbol adopted from Zia Pueblo is visible.

http://legis.state.nm.us/default.asp

(New Mexico Legislature)

BACK TOWARDS THE PLAZA

Turn right and walk down an alleyway toward the Santa Fe River. There is a walking path that parallels the river and East Alameda Street. Walk along this path, past the state Supreme Court until you come to Don Gaspar Avenue. Turn right on Don Gaspar and head back towards the Plaza. Formerly owned by Don Gaspar Ortiz y Alarid, this area was once an open field. Sr. Ortiz y Alarid lived in the northwest corner building at Don Gaspar and Water Street.

The Hotel St. Francis
210 Don Gaspar Avenue (and Water Street)

Originally the site of the Palace Hotel (built in the 1880s), the building burned completely to the ground in 1922. In 1924 it was rebuilt and

Looking east on San Francisco Street towards St. Francis Cathedral.

reopened as the De Vargas Hotel, a first-class hotel with a spacious lobby, a wonderful dining room and a bar. In the late 1920s, when Water Street was part of Route 66, the hotel was a favorite stopping-off place. Time took its toll, however, and the hotel was eventually sold in the 1980s and restored to its former Victorian glory, opening as the Hotel St. Francis. The St. Francis patio is a perfectly delightful spot for breakfast and lunch, and high tea in front of the lobby fireplace is not to be missed (see also page 99).

http://www.hotelstfrancis.com/
(Hotel St. Francis)
http://www.point-travel.com/santa-fe/hotel-st-francis.htm
(Hotel St. Francis history)

San Francisco Street

One of the city's oldest streets, San Francisco Street was the final destination at the end of the Camino Real (the King's Road) for covered wagons completing their 1,600-mile-journey from Mexico City.

http://www.elcaminoreal.org/flash/caminorealflash.htm
(El Camino Real)
http://www.sfaol.com/history/street.html
(Santa Fe's street names)

From the time the Spanish founded Santa Fe all goods came from Mexico City via the Camino Real. It was a long, hard and dangerous

Burro Alley is a pedestrian walkway. In summer its restaurants
sometimes feature outdoor dining here.

journey that ended as the wagons came up San Francisco Street and
unloaded on the Plaza. Historian Marc Simmons pointed out the haz-
ards in an article in *The New Mexican*:

> *The most dangerous stretch of the long Camino Real could be
> found in southern New Mexico. There it passed through the heart
> of Apacheria, as the homeland of the Apaches was called. Wagon
> trains expected to suffer casualties. In the Mesilla Valley one cara-
> van, after an attack, buried its dead at trailside. The next batch of
> travelers, noting the cluster of new marked graves, referred to the
> site as El Jardin de las Cruces (the Garden of the Crosses). Today's
> city of Las Cruces in its name continues to bear witness to that
> long-ago tragedy.*

http://www.asu.edu/lib/archives/schwarz/apacheria.htm
(Mission to Apachería)
http://www.oldmesilla.org/html/early_history.html
(Mesilla Valley early history)
http://www.lascrucescvb.org/html/history.html
(Las Cruces history)

Further west on this street is the Lensic Theater, built in 1931 as a legiti-
mate theater and movie house. Rita Hayworth, Roy Rogers and Judy

Garland all performed onstage at the Lensic. It was beautifully restored in 2001 and is now a prized venue for stage and dance venues, movies and lectures (see also page 52).

http://www.lensic.com/
(Lensic Theater)

Burro Alley

An historic 17th-century street adjacent to the Lensic is Burro Alley, the area once used to hitch burros needed for bringing wood down from the mountains. It is now a pedestrian walkway for retail shops and restaurants. A mural depicting the burros was done in the 1940s by Howard Kretz Coluzzi.

http://members.spinn.net/~squaredeal/history.html
(Old Square Deal shoeshop on Burro Alley)
http://www.santafestation.com/cafeparis/
(Café Paris restaurant on Burro Alley)

The Palace Restaurant
142 West Palace Avenue

At the end of Burro Alley on Palace Avenue sits the Palace Restaurant, once part of the "red light" district—the brothels, bars and saloons of San Francisco Street. Señora Doña Tules Barcelo owned the gambling hall that is now this restaurant (see also pages 79–80).

http://www.palacerestaurant.com/
(Palace Restaurant Web site)

Felipe B. Delgado House
124 West Palace Avenue

Continuing east on West Palace Avenue you will come to the Felipe B. Delgado House. Señor Delgado was a wealthy merchant in the wagon-train shipping business. After initially using this site as land to stable his mules, Delgado built his house here in 1890. Modified in the early 20th century, it remains an excellent example of local adobe construction, and it is authentically Territorial in style. It was used as a private residence until it was sold in 1970. It is currently occupied by a local bank.

http://www.historicsantafe.com/Delgado%20House.htm
(Felipe B. Delgado House)
http://perso.wanadoo.fr/rancho.pancho/Felipito.htm
(Felipe B. Delgado y Garcia)

The Museum of Fine Arts was constructed in typical Spanish style
around a central courtyard.

Museum of Fine Arts
107 West Palace Avenue

Diagonally across from the Delgado House stands the Museum of Fine
Arts, one of many superb museums in town. The Museum of Fine Arts
houses a collection of more than 20,000 works of art, including paintings, photography, sculpture and works on paper relating primarily to
the American Southwest (see page 63).

http://www.nmculture.org/
(New Mexico's Cultural Treasures site, click on index)
http://www.tfaoi.com/newsm1/n1m68.htm
(shows at the Museum of Fine Arts)
http://www.museumofnewmexico.org/
(Museums of New Mexico, click on Museum of Fine Arts)

The architecture firm of Rapp and Rapp constructed this building in
Spanish Pueblo Revival style. Completed in 1917, it also houses the St.
Francis Auditorium, designed to look like a pueblo church interior. The
wall mural panels were done by Carlos Vierra (1876–1937), the first
artist of any note to move here permanently (1904). Included in the
Fine Arts permanent collection are works by such artists as Georgia
O'Keeffe, Ernest Blumenschein and John Sloan.

http://architecture.about.com/library/bl-pueblo.htm
(Pueblo Revival style architecture)
http://jan.ucc.nau.edu/~twp/architecture/pueblo/
(Pueblo Revival style architecture pictures)
http://www.askart.com/artist/V/carlos_vierra.asp
(Carlos Vierra info)

Continuing to walk east on West Palace Avenue, you return to your starting point at the Palace of the Governors. Make sure you look at the window on the corner of Lincoln and Palace Avenues. The bars on these windows are made of gun barrels!

A VIRTUAL WALKING TOUR

The following link will take you on a virtual tour:
http://www.santafescene.com/walking-tour/
(a walking tour on the Web, with photos)
http://www.santafescene.com/walking-tour/background.htm
(history of Santa Fe and more details about the above virtual tour)

Ristras, bunches of red chiles strung up to dry, are
common decorative elements around town.

TOURS, TOURS, TOURS

As a docent for the Palace of the Governors I know the value of accurate, shared information, and I really recommend that you take at least one guided tour while you're here. The tour could focus on any number of personal-interest areas such as history, art, architecture, Indian art and culture or ghosts. Plan on spending an hour or two with your guide.

TOURS ON WHEELS

Custom Tours by Clarice
(505) 438-7116
Daily at 9 A.M., 11 A.M., 1 P.M., 3 P.M., 5 P.M.
Reservations recommended.
$10 per person, $5 per child under 12 accompanied by adult.
http://www.santafecustomtours.com/
(Custom Tours by Clarice)

Fiesta Tours
(505) 983-1570
Daily at 9 A.M., 11 A.M., 1 P.M., 3 P.M., 5 P.M., 6:30 P.M.
$7 per person, $4 per child under 12 accompanied by adult.
http://www.krazykyote.net/santafe/html/fiesta_tours.html
(Fiesta Tours)

The Loretto Line
(505) 983-3701
$12 per person, $6 per child under 12 accompanied by adult.
http://www.visitsantafe.com/businesspage.cfm?businessid=2308
(Loretto Line Tours)

Left: Santa Fe Plaza in winter.

Santa Fe Detours City Tours
(800) DETOURS or (505) 983-6565
$10 per person for 1½ hours.
$30 per person (includes admissions) for 3 hours.
http://www.sfdetours.com/tours.html
(Santa Fe Detours tours)

Open-air tour busses like this one provide a relaxing and informative
introduction to the sites around town.

WALKING TOURS

Aboot About Santa Fe Walking Tour
(505) 988-2774
Walking tours of downtown Santa Fe.
Twice daily.
$10 per person.

Aspook about Ghosts Tour
(505) 988-2774
Monday, Tuesday, Friday, Saturday at 5:30 P.M.
$10 per person.
http://www.abootabout.com/
(Aboot about Santa Fe and Aspook about Ghosts)
http://www.ghostinmysuitcase.com/places/santafe/
(Aspook about Ghosts tour)

Afoot in Santa Fe Walking Tours
(505) 983-3701
$10 per person; children under 16 accompanied by parent, free.
Daily at 9:30 A.M.
Starts at the Inn at Loretto (West Alameda Street and Old Santa Fe Trail).

Fine Arts Museum Art Walking Tour
107 West Palace Avenue
(505) 476-5072
Leaves from the museum steps at 107 West Palace Avenue every
Monday at 10 A.M., May through August.
This tour shows the art and architecture of the city.
$10 per person, children under 16 accompanied by adult, free.

Historic Walks of Santa Fe
(505) 986-8388
Historic Walks of Santa Fe offers a variety of types of tours. Some are
given all year round, but some only May through October. Call for
information. Some require reservations.

Historic Walks of Santa Fe
Walking tour of downtown Santa Fe.
Daily from La Fonda (on Plaza) at 9:45 A.M. and 1:15 P.M.
Daily from Plaza Galleria (on Plaza next to Simply Santa Fe)
at 10 A.M. and 1:30 P.M.
$10, children under 16 accompanied by adult are free, senior discount.

Ghostwalkers
The stories and legends of the ghosts of Santa Fe.
Starts every Friday from La Fonda lobby at 6 P.M.
$10 per person, reservations required.

Ghostwalkers Especial
A more in-depth Ghostwalker tour where "spirits come alive."
Starts every Friday from La Fonda lobby at 6 P.M.
$17.50 per person, 8-10 minimum, reservations required.

Santa Fe Art Gallery Tours
Tour of galleries, Museum of Fine Arts and
the Georgia O'Keeffe Museum with an expert.
Starts every Friday from La Fonda lobby at 2 P.M.
$16 per person (does not include museum admission fees).

Canyon Road Art Walks
Tour of Canyon Road historic buildings and important galleries.
Leaves from La Fonda lobby at 2 P.M.
$16 per person, $35 per person (includes lunch), reservations required.

Santa Fe Artists at Home
Special group tours to meet the artists of Santa Fe in their homes.
$65 per person includes transportation, reservations required.
Call for details.

Prestige Shopping Tour with Lunch
Half-day tour of some of Santa Fe's finest shops.
Price includes lunch at one of downtown's outstanding restaurants.
Reservations required, minimum of 4 people.
$35 per person (includes lunch).
http://www.historicwalksofsantafe.com/
(Historic Walks of Santa Fe)

History Talks, Palace Walks
(505) 476-5109
Tour of the Palace of the Governors and surrounding area.
Leaves from the blue gate of the Palace of the Governors
on Lincoln Avenue.
10:15 A.M. to noon, Monday–Saturday, May–October.
$10, children under 16 accompanied by adult, free.
Fees donated to the Palace of the Governors.
http://nmcn.org/features/walkingtours/
(Palace Walks, History Talks tour)

Santa Fe Detours
The Walking Tour of Santa Fe
(800) DETOURS or (505) 983-6565
Walking tour of historical downtown and the state capitol complex.
Starts daily from the T-shirt tree at 107 Washington Avenue on the
northeast corner of the Plaza at 9:30 A.M. and 1:30 P.M., 2½ hour tour.
$10 per person, $5 for children 12 and under.
http://www.sfdetours.com/tours.html
(Santa Fe Detours tours)

The courtyard gardens of Sena Plaza, a favorite stop of many tours.

CUSTOM TOURS

Art Colony Tours
(505) 466-6146
Local-color tours designed around your interests
(museums, galleries, opera, etc.).
Operates April–October, rest of year by arrangement.
Leaves at 9 A.M. and 1 P.M., hotel and downtown pickup.
$58 per person, minimum 4 people.
Call for reservations and information.
Out-of-town tours also available, call for details.

Taos
$95 per person, 9 hours

Bandelier
$75 per person, 9 hours

Abiquiú
$75 per person, 7 hours
http://www.artcolonytours.com/
(Art Colony Tours)

Santa Fe Detours Out-of-Town Tours
(800) DETOURS or (505) 983-6565
Half or full day tours, daily except Sunday.
Reservations required, pickup available.

Taos
$80 per person with children half price, all day.

Bandelier National Monument
$70 per person with children half price, half-day.

Puye Cliff Dwellings (includes Santa Clara Pueblo)
$70 per person with children half price, half day.

Custom tours
Hiking, biking, llama treks or private guides.
Call to make arrangements.
http://www.sfdetours.com/tours.html
(Santa Fe Detours tours)

Santa Fe Garden Club Home & Garden Tours

Behind Adobe Walls®
Summer bus tour of Santa Fe homes and gardens.
(505) 984-0022, Westwind Travel.
The last Tuesday in July and the first Tuesday in August.
$60 per person, reservations required.

Pequeño Tours
Santa Fe home and garden tour.
(505) 823-9030
April through October.
$45 per person, minimum of 10 people, reservations required.

Santa Fe Safaris
(888) 7-SAFARI
Half-day or full-day tours by four-wheel-drive vehicle, led by guides who are experienced in the natural history, culture and ecology of the area. See Web site for details about each safari.

Jemez Safari (includes Bandelier)
$85 (includes park fee and lunch), 6½ hours.

Taos Safari (includes Taos Pueblo and Santuario de Chimayó)
$96 (includes pueblo fee and lunch), all day.

Outback-Wildlife Safari (Jemez volcano area)
$65, evenings, 4½ hours.

Alpine Safari (Sangre de Cristo Mountains)
$48, 2½ hours.

*Turquoise Trail Sunset Safari (includes ghost towns,
petroglyphs, Madrid and Cerrillos),*
$55, departs afternoons, 3½ hours.

*O'Keeffe Country/Ghost Ranch Safari (includes Indian ruins
and Echo Amphitheater)*
$85 (includes lunch), 6½ hours.

Birds of Bosque del Apache Safari
(a paradise for birders especially in winter).
$115 (includes refuge fees and lunch), late morning to early evening.

Custom and Private Safaris
call to arrange your own custom safari.
http://www.outbacktours.com/santafe.html
(Santa Fe Safaris)

Santa Fe Tours
(505) 988-8022

The City Different:
A Walking Tour of Santa Fe
$12 per person, group rates available, time by arrangement.

Artists and Acequias:
A Cultural and Artistic Tour of Canyon Road and the East Side
$18 per person, group rates available.
Mondays at 10 A.M. or by appointment.

Bars and Brothels of Santa Fe:
A Red Light Tour
Check out the famous watering holes in town, both past and present.
$18 per person.
Wednesdays and Saturdays 7–9 P.M. winter; 8–10 P.M. summer.

The Dark Side of Santa Fe
Ghosts, Mysteries & Legends
Learn about the ghosts in public or private buildings
in this 400-year-old city.
$12 per person, $8 children, under 5 free.
Sundays and Thursdays at 5:30 and 7:30 P.M.

A History Different:
A Look at the Jewish Legacy in New Mexico
An overview tour of the Jewish whereabouts in the 19th century, the
hidden or Crypto-Jews and the present-day Jewish community.
$15 per person, Thursdays at 10 A.M.

Garden Tours:
Past & Present
Tour Santa Fe gardens in public buildings, galleries and private places
with a local gardener and historian.
$18 per person, Tuesdays at 10 A.M.
http://www.zianet.com/stebeni/santafetours2.htm
(Santa Fe Tours)

MUSEUM TOURS

Museums of New Mexico

Please see the chapter on museums (pages 61–71) for complete information regarding museum descriptions, hours of operation, museum
entry fees, etc. The information given here relates strictly to the guided
tours of each site. For updated information on the museums of New
Mexico, call their 24-hour information line, (505) 827-6463, or go to the
main Web site for the museum system:
http://www.museumofnewmexico.org/
(Museum of New Mexico)

Museum of Fine Arts
107 West Palace Avenue
(505) 476-5072
Docent tours: Tuesday–Sunday at 10:30 A.M. and 1:30 P.M.
Tour fee is included with $7 museum admission.
http://www.nmculture.org/
(New Mexico's Cultural Treasures site, click on index)

Palace of the Governors
105 West Palace Avenue
(505) 476-5100
Docent tours: Tuesday–Sunday at 10:30 A.M., noon, 1:30 P.M., 3 P.M.
Tour fee is included with $7 museum admission.
http://palaceofthegovernors.org/
(Palace of the Governors)

The Indian Market car, painted by Dan Namingha and decorated by nine Native American artists, is featured with Indian bronze statues in front of the Museum of Indian Arts & Culture.

Museum of Indian Arts & Culture
710 Camino Lejo
(505) 476-1250
Docent tour: First Saturday of the month at 2 P.M.
Tour fee is included with $7 museum admission.
http://www.miaclab.org/indexfl.html
(Museum of Indian Arts & Culture)

Museum of International Folk Art
706 Camino Lejo
(505) 476-1200
Docent tour: Tuesdays and Wednesdays at 10:15 A.M. and 2 P.M.
Thursdays through Sundays at 10:15 A.M., 1 P.M. and 3 P.M.
Tour fee is included with $7 museum admission.
http://www.moifa.org/
(Museum of International Folk Art)
http://www.nmoca.com/
(New Mexico Office of Cultural Affairs)

DIVAS & DIVERSIONS

Richard Bradford (1933–2002), author of *Red Sky at Morning*, once said of Santa Fe: "At age 12, within 15 minutes of coming here, I realized that I'd been making a terrible mistake living in large urban centers. This was the place for me. I felt immediately at home; I have never felt so quickly, so comfortably, so deeply attracted."—From *Turn Left at the Sleeping Dog* by John Pen la Farge.

Santa Fe is a town of incredible cultural diversity. We are thrilled to share world-class offerings in all kinds of music, including classical (opera, chamber music, orchestra and choral music), jazz, flamenco, country, bluegrass and world beat, as well as popular artists who come to entertain under the stars at our local outdoor venues in the summer. Santa Fe has its own stage shows and plays host to traveling theater groups as well as ballet, international and modern dance groups that come to town.

In addition to all our outstanding restaurants, we have a variety of other attractions, including a farmer's market that ranks with the best in the country, a flea market where a myriad of items are sold at bargain prices and an old-time railroad train that takes you on an excursion through the spectacular scenery of the desert Southwest.

http://nmculturenet.org/artists
(CultureNetWork, an on-line directory of artists, artisans, arts organizations, galleries and others involved in the cultural life of New Mexico)
http://www.newmexico.org/
(New Mexico Department of Tourism, statewide attractions and maps)
http://www.santafe.org/
(Santa Fe Convention and Visitors Bureau)
http://www.collectorsguide.com/sf/sffa01.html
(intro to Santa Fe)

Left: One of the many classical music events held aat the Lensic Performing Arts Center. Photo ©Sam Adams.

http://www.santafe.com/
(Santa Fe On Line Magazine, listings and reviews of accommodations and restaurants with addresses and phone numbers, also attractions and the arts)

http://www.visitsantafe.com/
(listings and links for accommodations and restaurants, sorted by type, also activities, the arts and maps)

http://www.thesantafesite.com/
(listings and some links for accommodations and restaurants, events and outdoor activities, also some features relating to Santa Fe subjects)

http://www.sfaol.com/
(similar to above sites, contains a wider variety of links)

http://www.santafeinformation.com/
(similar to other general information sites above, but includes a Web cam)

http://www.nmmagazine.com/
(Web site for New Mexico Magazine, statewide attractions and features, also Internet links sorted by category, including over 1,000 for Santa Fe alone)

http://www.santafean.com/
(Web site for the Santa Fean magazine, contains features relating specifically to Santa Fe, especially art and culture, also selected local links)

SOME OF THE FINEST CLASSICAL MUSIC

The Santa Fe Opera
Approximately 7 miles north of Santa Fe on U.S. 84/285
(800) 280-4654 or (505) 986-5900
Season: late June to late August

In 1980, my wife, Mary, and I came to Santa Fe for the first time. Although we were not opera fans, we had heard so much about The Santa Fe Opera that we got tickets for Mozart's *The Magic Flute.* I must say that being in the opera house, viewing the sunset over Los Alamos and watching the stars appear as the desert breeze wafted in while we listened to the overture was a truly delightful, multi-sensory experience. We became opera lovers that night.

Santa Feans have been treated to the opera since John Crosby inaugurated it in 1957. Mr. Crosby served as the company's general director from its founding in 1957 until 2000 when he retired. He passed on in 2002, at the age of 76.

Situated on a former guest ranch seven miles north of Santa Fe, the opera house is acoustically perfect. Originally, there were 480 seats under the stars. 1998 saw the construction of a new 2,128-seat theater

An evening at The Santa Fe Opera is an experience you will never forget.
Photo ©Robert Reck/The Santa Fe Opera.

partially covered by a roof. Call for a schedule and tickets before you
arrive in town, as most nights are sellouts. You can also order tickets
from the opera Web site.

Although the season runs from late June to late August, some
nights are cool and some seats are not fully covered. It is always wise to
bring rain gear.

http://www.santafeopera.org/
(The Santa Fe Opera)
http://www.festivalsantafe.org/
(central Web site for classical performances in Santa Fe)

Santa Fe Chamber Music Festival
239 Johnson Street, office
Performances at various venues
(505) 983-2075
For tickets only, in summer—(505) 982-1890
Season: mid-July to end of August

Since 1972 the Chamber Music Festival has been a mainstay of the classical music scene in Santa Fe. From mid-July to the end of August, the festival presents over forty concerts at St. Francis Auditorium and at the newly renovated Lensic Performing Arts Center, featuring world-class musicians such as Pinchas Zuckerman, Cho-Liang Lin and the Orion String Quartet.

Supplementing the evening concerts, one-hour noon concerts are presented at the St. Francis Auditorium for a cost of $10. These noon concerts are among the most popular recitals in Santa Fe.

In addition to traditional classical music, jazz, new "cutting edge" classical and world music are also part of the programming of the festival.

http://www.santafechambermusic.org/
(Santa Fe Chamber Music Festival)
http://lensic.com/events.html
(event schedule at the Lensic Performing Arts Center)
http://www.festivalsantafe.org/
(central Web site for classical performances in Santa Fe)

Santa Fe Desert Chorale
Performances at various venues
(505) 988-2282 or (800) 244-4011

Season: end of June to mid-August, then during Christmas season. If you enjoy chorale music, you will love the Desert Chorale. Initiated in 1983, it represents the finest in chamber chorus singing. One evening, at the acoustically perfect Loretto Chapel, we listened to a mesmerizing blend of ancient Hebrew psalms and Gregorian chants that came off beautifully. The Chorale performs not only at the Loretto Chapel, but also at the Lensic Performing Arts Center, Santa María de la Paz Catholic Community and the St. Francis Cathedral.

http://www.desertchorale.org/
(Santa Fe Desert Chorale)
http://lensic.com/events.html
(event schedule at the Lensic Performing Arts Center)

Santa Fe Pro Musica
Performances at the Lensic Performing Arts Center
211 West San Francisco Street
(800) 960-6680 or (505) 988-4640
Season: year round

Santa Fe Pro Musica was established in 1994 to present classical concerts of the highest quality consistent with international standards of excellence. Locally based, Santa Fe Pro Musica provides both orchestral and chamber music offerings, specializing in music from the nineteenth century and before. Using its unique affiliation with the Smithsonian Institution, Santa Fe Pro Musica uses period instruments whenever possible. A complete schedule is available at its Web site.

http://www.santafepromusica.com/
(Santa Fe Pro Musica)
http://lensic.com/events.html
(event schedule at the Lensic Performing Arts Center)

Santa Fe Symphony and Chorus
551 West Cordova Road, Suite D, office
Performances at the Lensic Performing Arts Center
211 W. San Francisco Street
(800) 480-1319 or (505) 983-1414
Season: year round

Santa Fe has its own symphony orchestra performing a variety of classical traditions from Handel and Beethoven to Dvorak and Copland. Some performances also showcase classical Spanish and jazz crossover styles. Call for schedule.

http://www.sf-symphony.org/
(Santa Fe Symphony and Chorus)
http://lensic.com/events.html
(event schedule at the Lensic Performing Arts Center)

MUSICAL AND THEATRICAL OFFERINGS FOR EVERY TASTE

For more ideas, see the calendar of events starting on page 197.

María Benítez Teatro Flamenco

Performances at the Radisson Hotel, 750 North St. Francis Drive
(888) 4-FLAMENCO or (505) 955-8562
Season: late June to late August

Under the artistic direction of María and Cecilio Benítez, this company of professional dancers and musicians presents diverse and demanding performances of music and dance showcasing the rhythms of flamenco. Teatro Flamenco performers come from throughout the United States and Spain. Recognized as one of the nation's leading performing arts groups, Teatro Flamenco also appears at New York's Joyce Theatre, Lincoln Center, and the Kennedy Center in Washington. Teatro Flamenco aims to preserve, strengthen and disseminate the rich and diverse artistic heritage of Spain, enriching the lives not only of people of Spanish ancestry, but of all Americans.

http://www.mariabenitez.com/
(María Benítez Teatro Flamenco and the Institute for Spanish Arts
http://www.festivalsantafe.org/
(central Web site for classical performances in Santa Fe)

Santa Fe Playhouse

142 East De Vargas Street
(505) 983-4262

Founded in 1922, the Santa Fe Playhouse is the oldest continuously running theater company west of the Mississippi. It is distinguished by being housed in an historic adobe building in the Barrio de Analco (see page 26) and is noted for the annual *Fiesta Melodrama*, a spoof and satire on the City Different. As was intended by founder Mary Austin, the Playhouse is dedicated to presenting works that give voice to Santa Fe's many cultures and communities. The Playhouse offers a variety of theater year round with musicals, comedies, dramas, murder-mysteries and classics.

http://www.santafeplayhouse.org/
(Santa Fe Playhouse)

Combine history and culture with a visit to the Santa Fe Playhouse.

Santa Fe Stages
Most performances at the Lensic Performing Arts Center
211 West San Francisco Street
Some performances at the Armory for the Arts, 1050 Old Pecos Trail
(505) 982-6683
Season: May through October

Founded in 1995, Santa Fe Stages is committed to bringing world-class theater to New Mexico audiences and is the area's primary presenter of modern dance. Santa Fe Stages also offers a wide variety of cutting-edge theater, solo performance art, cabaret and world music.

http://www.santafestages.org/
(Santa Fe Stages)
http://www.festivalsantafe.org/
(central Web site for classical performances in Santa Fe)
http://lensic.com/events.html
(event schedule at the Lensic Performing Arts Center)

With its excellent acoustics and "no bad seats," the Lensic Performing Arts Center has become the venue of choice for a wide variety of theatrical and musical performances.

Lensic Performing Arts Center
211 West San Francisco Street
Box office: (505) 988-1234

Originally opened in 1931 as a film and vaudeville palace, the Lensic Theatre was remodeled in 2000 and reopened as a world-class, state-of-the-art, 821-seat venue—an ideal space for chamber music, theater, modern dance, flamenco, ballet, jazz, operetta, film and poetry. Beautifully restored, the Lensic Performing Arts Center boasts perfect acoustics and "not a bad seat in the house." It is now the venue of choice for many local and national productions. You can check the Lensic Web site to find out what is happening during the week you plan to be in town. You cannot purchase tickets from this site, but you can look at a seating chart and use one of the links provided to purchase tickets directly from the organization holding the performance. Or, of course, you can call the box office and purchase tickets there.

http://lensic.com/
(Lensic Performing Arts Center)

Piano Bar at Vanessie Restaurant
434 West San Francisco Street
(505) 982-9966

Enjoy dinner or just stop by for dessert or a drink and enjoy live music from Santa Fe's only piano bar. Some of the patrons even get up to sing and dance!

http://www.nmrestaurants.com/Vanessie/
(Vanessie Restaurant and Piano Bar)

OTHER VENUES FOR NATIONAL ACTS

Several other venues draw national music acts from rock to jazz to country. Check these Web sites to see who may be playing when you come to town. Also, check the newspapers and fliers about town for other venues as well as the club scene.

Paolo Soleri Amphitheater
1501 Cerrillos Road

This beautifully designed, acoustically wonderful outdoor venue draws national acts every summer.

http://www.jambase.com/search.asp?venueID=166
(Paolo Soleri Amphitheater tickets)
http://www.ticketmaster.com/venue/245996/
(Paolo Soleri Amphitheater tickets)

Journal Pavilion
Off I-25 south of Albuquerque
(505) 246-8742

The large rock acts play here. It is easy to get to, just south of Albuquerque and about an hour from Santa Fe. The easiest way to go is to follow the directions on the Pavilion Web site. You will also find a schedule, and you can purchase tickets there as well.

http://www.journalpavilion.com/
(Journal Pavilion)

Casinos

Many of the Indian casinos bring in name acts, Las Vegas style. They usually feature classic rock, country, comedy and nightclub acts. They advertise on their billboards, on TV and in the paper. You can also check the Web sites of the individual casinos offering events (see pages 188–90).

OTHER UNIQUE DIVERSIONS

Santa Fe Farmers' Market
430 West Manhattan Street, in the Railyard Park
near train depot off Guadalupe Street
(505) 983-4098

This unique open-air farmers' market had its beginnings in 1976. *Sunset Magazine* named it one of the best in the Southwest. Hispanic growers, whose land has been in their families for centuries, bring apples, chiles, vegetables, salsa and jams to the market. They stand alongside young Anglo farmers who love the land as well and harvest their bounty for all of us. Most of the market sellers are certified organic growers. During harvest time, the market is buzzing at 7 A.M. with coffee and pastry vendors at the ready to satisfy early shoppers. Bands, guitar players and country violins appear on a catch-as-catch-can basis. In July and August, Jake from Fort Summer brings in corn and melons of various varieties, and many people swear they're the best they've ever tasted. Here at the market you meet the residents of Santa Fe, so don't be surprised if you're invited to someone's home for drinks that night. In the winter, you may find many market products at El Museo Cultural de Santa Fe in the Railyard Park complex.

http://www.farmersmarketsnm.org/santafe/index.htm
(Santa Fe Farmers' Market)
http://www.tradenm.org/directory/2a2.html#1
(Farmers' markets in New Mexico)

Tesuque Pueblo Flea Market
About 7 miles north of Santa Fe on U.S. 84/285 near the Opera
(505) 995-8626
Open every Friday, Saturday and Sunday.

Called Trader Jack's when it first opened in the 1980s, the flea market has grown each year. Now run by the Tesuque Pueblo on its land, it offers a fascinating mix of merchandise sold by equally fascinating individuals. In the stalls of the 200 permanent vendors, you'll find both Native American and contemporary jewelry, clothing, oriental rugs, antiques, woodwork, furniture, local food, jams, salsa, art, photography and more. Wear sunglasses, a hat and some comfortable, closed walking shoes.

http://www.tesuquepueblofleamarket.com/
(Tesuque Pueblo Flea Market official site)

http://www.visitsantafe.com/businesspage.cfm?businessid=1607
(Tesuque Pueblo Flea Market)
http://www.sfaol.com/best/fleamarket.html
(Tesuque Pueblo Flea Market)
http://www.azcentral.com/travel/destinations/newmexico/articles/tesuque.html
(Tesuque Pueblo Flea Market)

The authentically restored coaches of the Santa Fe Southern Railway provide a relaxing way to experience some high-desert scenery with a bit of history as well.

Ride the Old Train to Lamy

Santa Fe Southern Railway at 410 South Guadalupe Street
(505) 989-8600 or (888) 989-8600

Even though most of us are familiar with the railway name, "the Atchison, Topeka and Santa Fe," it's a lesser-known fact that Santa Fe was actually not on the main route of that railway. It was merely a spur line. The main stop was at Las Vegas, New Mexico. Nonetheless, you can take a day ride on that spur line to Lamy—named for Archbishop Lamy, who used the quarry in that town to supply stone for St. Francis Cathedral.

http://digital.library.arizona.edu/harvey/finding_aid/8nm/1/welcome.html
(El Ortiz Hotel in Lamy)
http://www.huntel.com/~artpike/lamy1.htm
(old Lamy, NM photos)

This round-trip journey on a vintage coach takes about 4¼ hours— hours well spent viewing the ever-changing New Mexican landscape while comfortably seated on a train. In Lamy, you can get lunch at Marianna's at the Depot (except Sunday and Monday), or you may bring a picnic. You'll experience the vast, breathtaking beauty of New Mexico with a minimum expenditure of effort. Call for exact departure times and cost.

http://sfsr.com/daytrain.html
(Santa Fe Southern Railway day train)
http://sfsr.com/
(Santa Fe Southern Railway, all trains)
http://www.santafescene.com/sfs/
(Santa Fe Southern detailed schedules)

CANYON ROAD WALK

All the guidebooks and travel agents tell you to make sure you walk Canyon Road to see the art galleries. Thankfully, Canyon Road has survived its onslaught of tourists and has not become a "theme" street devoid of sensibility.

Canyon Road has gone through its own realities, first as a Pueblo Indian footpath, then as a road the Spanish called El Camino de Canyon (Canyon Road). Spaniards built modest homes here early in the 20th century, and artists migrated to the road because of its low rent and pleasant vistas.

Interspersed among private adobe residences, art galleries and shops, occasional restaurants or coffee shops in several historic houses provide lunches and fine dining.

Every Friday evening many of the galleries on Canyon Road hold show openings. This Friday night walk is an enjoyable way to see the art, meet the artists, and enjoy refreshments in the cool Santa Fe evening.

Another special Canyon Road walk is held every year on Christmas Eve. Brightly burning *farolitos* line Canyon Road and several side streets, as thousands of Santa Feans walk and mingle about, enjoying the holiday decorations, greeting friends and singing carols. Bonfires and hot apple cider warm bodies and souls. The smell of the burning piñon logs will forever linger in your memory. Be sure to dress warmly.

http://goamericanwest.com/newmexico/santafe/sfcanyonroad.shtml
(articles on Canyon Road)
http://www.desertusa.com/mag00/jul/stories/croad.html
(Santa Fe's Beguiling Canyon Road)

A typical Canyon Road gateway.

First Ward School
400 Canyon Road

Once in a while you come across a Santa Fe building that is neither Pueblo Revival nor Territorial style, and you may ask What style is it? The First Ward School is constructed of kilned brick rather than adobe and is of the Neoclassical style. It was built as a public school house in 1906 to someday replace the Loretto and St. Michael schools built by Archbishop Lamy, but in fact it never did. Twenty-two years after the school's completion, the city sold it. It has undergone several incarnations and is now one of the many art galleries on Canyon Road.

El Zaguan
545 Canyon Road

This architectural gem was built in 1849 by James Johnson and features an unusual garden west of the house. Designed by Adolph Bandelier (Bandelier National Monument is named for him) in a formal Victorian style, the garden has 100-year-old peony bushes and two large chestnut trees. The house itself grew over the years, including the addition of a covered passageway, or "zaguan," from which addition the house derived its name. The house is now owned by the Historic Santa Fe Foundation, and its interior has been converted into rental apartments.

http://www.historicsantafe.com/El%20Zaguan.htm

(El Zaguan)

Canyon Road is known for its historical buildings as well as its galleries.

Olive Rush Studio
630 Canyon Road

Olive Rush, who arrived in 1920, was one of the first female artists to live in Santa Fe. Little is known about the age of this house, but it is estimated that it was built in the early 1800s. Because Olive was a Quaker (the Society of Friends) the house was deeded to them and is lovingly maintained to this day.

http://artarchives.si.edu/htgmonth/amerind/rush.htm
(Olive Rush)

Rafael Borrego House
724 Canyon Road

Part of this very old house can be traced back to 1753 and reveals that it was typical of upscale homes of that era. Over the years rooms and refinements were added, including the Territorial portal now used by Geronimo restaurant (see page 86) for outdoor dining in the summer months. The restaurant is named after Geronimo Lopez, one of the house's first owners.

http://www.epicurious.com/erg/santafe/geronimo.html
(Geronimo restaurant)
http://www.historicsantafe.com/Registry.htm
(Registry of Resources)

Cristo Rey Catholic Church bears the unmistakable stamp of its famous architect, John Gaw Meem.

Cristo Rey Catholic Church
Canyon Road at Camino Cabra

This relatively new adobe church was built in 1940 to commemorate the 400th anniversary of Coronado's presence in New Mexico. Congregation members made the adobe bricks, about 200,000 of them, and helped to build the church. John Gaw Meem, an outstanding Santa Fe architect, designed it in the Spanish Mission style. One stunning feature of the church is the stone altar screen, originally carved in 1760 for the military chapel, La Castrense, located opposite the Palace of the Governors on the Plaza. The main saint depicted is Santiago—St. James —the patron saint of Spain.

http://www.paete.org/abtpaete/pafiesta.htm
(feast of St. James)
http://www.kfki.hu/~arthp/html/g/greco_el/1606-10/apostola/03jamesg.html
(St. James portrait by Greco)
http://www.spanishcolonial.org/johngawmeem.shtml
(Spanish Pueblo Revival style—John Gaw Meem)
http://www.cristoreycatholicchurch.org/
(Cristo Rey Catholic Church)

MUSEUMS

Imagine a city of about 70,000 people with sixteen museums! That's probably a record of sorts, and there's good reason for this number. Santa Fe is both a historic city and an art community that draws from three cultures contributing to its unique creative style.

DOWNTOWN

In or near the Plaza area you'll find five museums to enjoy, each emphasizing both history and art.

Archdiocese of Santa Fe Museum
223 Cathedral Place
(505) 983-3811
Open Monday–Friday, 9 A.M.–4 P.M.
Donation requested

After touring the St. Francis Cathedral itself and viewing its collection of religious artifacts, you'll find a small museum that those interested in Santa Fe history will find appealing. Among the exhibits are Archbishop Lamy's boar-hair trunk, the golden chalice given to him by Pope Pius IX in 1854, a relic of the "True Cross."

http://www.nmculturenet.org/artists/Detailed/2124.html
(Archdiocese of Santa Fe Museum)
http://www.evanderputten.org/special/newmexico/sfcathedral.htm
(St. Francis Cathedral)

left: The Museum of Fine Arts.

The Awakening Museum
125 N. Guadalupe Street
(505) 989-7636
Open 10 a.m.–6 p.m.daily summer, 10 a.m.–5 p.m. daily winter.
Adults $3, children (12 and under) and students free,
Fridays New Mexico residents (with ID) and seniors free.

Unique and inspiring, this ecumenical museum permanently houses a
monumental narrative artwork carved, then painted with dazzling shapes
and colors on hundreds of wood panels by artist Jean-Claude Gaugy.

http://www.theawakeningmuseum.org/
(The Awakening Museum)

The Georgia O'Keeffe Museum
211 Johnson Street
(505) 995-0785
Open 10 A.M.–5 P.M. daily.
Adults $8, New Mexico residents (with ID) $4.
5 P.M.–8 P.M. on Fridays only, free.

The Georgia O'Keeffe Museum is the only museum in Santa Fe devoted
to a single woman artist. Located in a small building remodeled from
an old church, the museum presents a spare, indeed Spartan ambiance
that helps to illuminate the artist and her work. This private museum
opened in 1997 and is well worth a visit. The museum contains nine
galleries, some showing O'Keeffe's work only, and some her work combined with that of her contemporaries from other collections to
demonstrate the significance of her achievement within the history of
modern American art.

http://www.okeeffemuseum.org/indexflash.php
(The Georgia O'Keeffe Museum)
http://www.georgiaokeeffe.com/
(Georgia O'Keeffe Web site)
http://www.artcyclopedia.com/artists/okeeffe_georgia.html
(Georgia O'Keeffe Artcyclopedia)

Institute of American Indian Arts Museum
108 Cathedral Place
(505) 983-8900
June–September: Monday–Saturday, 9 A.M.–5 P.M.,
Sunday, 10 A.M.–5 P.M.

The Institute of American Indian Arts Museum showcases the work
of its students as well as established masters.

October–May: Monday–Saturday, 10 A.M.–5 P.M.,
Sunday, noon–5 P.M.
Adults $4, seniors (62 and over) $2, students $2,
children under 16 and members free.

This museum of contemporary Indian arts opened in 1992. The former
Federal Building (the post office) was renovated to create a venue for
Indian artists from not only the Southwest but all over the country. A
sculpture garden in the back features the work of renowned Chiricahua
Apache sculptor Allan Houser.

http://www.iaiancad.org/
(Institute of American Indian Arts)
http://www.allanhouserfoundation.org/
(Allan Houser Foundation)

Museum of Fine Arts
107 West Palace Avenue
(505) 476-5072
24-hour recorded information: (505) 827-6463
Open Tuesday–Sunday, 10 A.M.–5 P.M.
$7 per person for one visit, one museum, one day only.
$15 four-day pass, unlimited visits, all five museums of New Mexico.
New Mexico residents $5, free all day Sunday and 5 P.M.–8 P.M. Friday.
New Mexico senior citizens also free on Wednesdays.
Children 16 and younger, always free.

This venerable art museum was founded in 1917. The museum's permanent collection of Santa Fe and Taos painters includes work by Georgia O'Keeffe, John Sloan and Ernest Blumenschein. Additionally, several exhibits each year feature the cutting edge of contemporary painting. Free tours with a docent are available (see also page 42).

http://www.museumofnewmexico.org/about.html
(Museums of New Mexico)
http://www.museumofnewmexico.org/
(Museums of New Mexico, click on Museum of Fine Arts)
http://www.nmculture.org/
(New Mexico's Cultural Treasures site, click on index)

Palace of the Governors
100 Palace Avenue
(505) 476-5100
24-hour recorded information: (505) 827-6463
Open Tuesday–Sunday, 10 A.M.–5 P.M.
$7 per person for one visit, one museum, one day only.
$15 four-day pass, unlimited visits, all five museums of New Mexico.
New Mexico residents: $5, free all day Sunday and 5 P.M.–8 P.M. Friday.
New Mexico senior citizens also free on Wednesdays.
Children 16 and younger, always free.

Built in 1610, the Palace of the Governors is the oldest continuously used government building in the United States. In 1912, it became the History Museum of New Mexico. Inside you will find Spanish and Indian artifacts, a portrait gallery of those who shaped Santa Fe, a chapel, and a courtyard housing historic wagons. In about 2005, a new contemporary wing is to be added to include some of the treasures now languishing in the basement. Free tours with a docent are available and offer an overview of New Mexico history from ancient times to the present (see also page 42).

http://palaceofthegovernors.org/
(Palace of the Governors)
http://www.museumofnewmexico.org/about.html
(Museums of New Mexico)
http://www.museumofnewmexico.org/
(Museums of New Mexico, click on Palace of the Governors)
http://www.nmculture.org/HTML/direct.htm
(click on Museum of New Mexico, then on Palace of the Governors)

JUST OFF THE PLAZA

The Santuario de Guadalupe is still used today for weddings,
funerals and musical events.

Santuario de Guadalupe
100 South Guadalupe Street
(505) 988-2027

Just a short distance from the Plaza is the historic Nuestra Señora de
Guadalupe church, now used mainly as an art and history museum.
Built in 1781, the Santuario houses the Archdiocese of Santa Fe's collec-
tion of New Mexican *santos* (carved images of the saints), Italian
Renaissance paintings, and Mexican baroque paintings. Among the
treasured works is *Our Lady of Guadalupe,* one of the largest and finest
oil paintings of the Spanish Southwest, dated 1783 and signed by José de
Alzibar, one of Mexico's most renowned painters.

http://www.nmculture.org/
(New Mexico's Cultural Treasures site, click on index)
http://www.umilta.net/pure.html
(image of Our Lady of Guadalupe *painting)*

Indian Arts Research Center
At the School of American Research
660 Garcia Street
(505) 954-7205

This collection is only open for viewing on Fridays at 2 P.M. with a
docent-guided tour. $15 per person, advance reservations only.

The School of American Research is little-known by most tourists but is an absolute treasure source for collectors, researchers and scholars. It houses one of the most significant collections of traditional Southwest Indian arts and artifacts, spanning the 450-year period from Spanish contact to the present. Complemented by beautiful landscaping, this Spanish Pueblo Revival-style building was once the home of newspaper heiress Amelia White, who bequeathed it to the school in 1972. Its collection of 11,000 artifacts includes pottery, textiles, paintings, basketry, jewelry and ethnographic materials.

http://www.sarweb.org/ie4.htm
(School of American Research main site)
http://www.sarweb.org/iarc/tours.htm
(School of American Research tours)

MUSEUM HILL

Drive south on Old Santa Fe Trail, being sure you stay to the left when the road forks. About 1½ miles from the Plaza you will come to Camino Lejo. Make a right and you'll be in the museum cluster. After parking, you will enter the Milner Plaza (completed in 2001), which leads to three of the museums.

http://www.museumhill.org/
(Museum Hill Web site)

Museum of Indian Arts and Culture
The Laboratory of Anthropology
710 Camino Lejo
(505) 476-1250
24-hour recorded information: (505) 827-6463
Open Tuesday–Sunday, 10 A.M.–5 P.M.
$7 per person for one visit, one museum, one day only.
$15 four-day pass, unlimited visits, all five museums of New Mexico.
New Mexico residents $5, free all day Sunday and 5 P.M.–8 P.M. Friday.
New Mexico senior citizens also free on Wednesdays.
Children 16 and younger, always free.

Across the Milner Plaza is a museum built in 1986 to display artifacts from Native cultures. Housing over 50,000 pieces of textiles, clothing, pottery and basketry, it is a treasure trove of the ancient Southwest. Free tours with a docent are available.

http://www.miaclab.org/visit/index.html
(Museum of Indian Arts and Culture)

http://www.museumofnewmexico.org/about.html
(Museums of New Mexico)
http://www.nmculture.org/
(New Mexico's Cultural Treasures site, click on index)
http://www.museumofnewmexico.org/
(Museums of New Mexico, click on Museum of Indian Arts and Culture)

Museum of International Folk Art
706 Camino Lejo
(505) 476-1200
24-hour recorded information: (505) 827-6463
Open Tuesday–Sunday, 10 A.M.–5 P.M.
$7 per person for one visit, one museum, one day only.
$15 four-day pass, unlimited visits, all five museums of New Mexico.
New Mexico residents $5, free all day Sunday and 5 P.M.–8 P.M. Friday.
New Mexico senior citizens also free on Wednesdays.
Children 16 and younger, always free.

This is one of the most unique museums in the country. Founded in 1953 by Florence Dibell Bartlett to show off her folk art collection, the museum enjoyed a significant increase in prestige with the acquisition in the 1980s of the Alexander Girard collection. Mr. Girard was a designer who loved primitive folk art, and his collection is an exquisite tribute to that genre. Young and old alike will love this fanciful section of the museum. In 1989, the Hispanic Heritage Wing was added to focus on folk art of the Southwest. Additionally, in 1999, Lloyd Cotzen donated the funds to build the Neutrogena Wing to house his collection of 5,000 artifacts and textiles from around the world, with items shown on a revolving basis. Free tours with a docent are available.

http://www.moifa.org/
(Museum of International Folk Art)
http://www.museumofnewmexico.org/about.html
(Museums of New Mexico)
http://www.nmculture.org/
(New Mexico's Cultural Treasures site, click on index)
http://www.museumofnewmexico.org/
(Museums of New Mexico, click on Museum of International Folk Art)

Milner Plaza, on Museum Hill, featuring the Apache Dancer statue, includes the Museum of Indian Arts and Culture, the Museum of International Folk Art, the Laboratory of Anthropology and the Museum Hill Café. The Wheelwright Museum of the American Indian and the Museum of Spanish Colonial Arts are also located on Museum Hill.

Wheelwright Museum of the American Indian
704 Camino Lejo
(505) 982-4636
Open Monday–Saturday, 10 A.M.–5 P.M., Sunday, 1 P.M.–5 P.M.
Free admission.

Near the museum cluster run by the Museum of New Mexico Foundation is the private Wheelwright Museum. It was founded in 1937 by Mary Cabot Wheelwright and Navajo medicine man Hosteen Klah (1867–1937). A small gem of a museum, it's eight-sided, shaped like a "hogan," or traditional Navajo home. Seasonally changing exhibitions in the main gallery include contemporary and traditional American Indian art, with an emphasis on the Southwest.

http://www.wheelwright.org/
(Wheelwright Museum of the American Indian)
http://www.lapahie.com/Hosteen_Klah.cfm
(Hosteen Klah, "Sir Left Handed")
http://coralcoast.com/art/articles/Cultural.Art/Navajho.Sand.Paintings.html
(Hosteen Klah and Navajo sand paintings)

Museum of Spanish Colonial Arts
750 Camino Lejo
(505) 982-2226
Open Tuesday–Sunday, 10 A.M.–5 P.M.
Adults $6, children 17 and under free, New Mexico residents, $3.

Heading back on Camino Lejo to the Old Santa Fe Trail, consider making your last stop the newest museum in Santa Fe. Opened in July of 2002, this compact, unique museum is built around a John Gaw Meem home and houses a collection of Spanish colonial furniture as well as art and artifacts including straw applique, pottery, wooden furniture, tinwork, and of course, carved saints (*santos* in Spanish). The collection spans the Middle Ages to the present. Free tours with a docent are available.

http://www.spanishcolonial.org/
(Museum of Spanish Colonial Art)

Museum Hill Café
710 Camino Lejo
(505) 820-1776
Tuesday through Sunday, 9 A.M.–3 P.M.
Luncheon, 11 A.M.–3 P.M.

If you feel you can't go on without sustenance of some sort—some coffee perhaps, or a sandwich—take heart, the Museum Hill Café is close at hand!

http://www.museumhill.org/dine.html
(Museum Hill Café)

FOR THE LATEST IN CONTEMPORARY ART

SITE Santa Fe
1606 Paseo de Peralta
(505) 989-1199
Open Wednesday–Sunday, 10 A.M.–5 P.M.
Friday, 10 A.M.–7 P.M.
Adults $5, seniors and students $2.50, Friday free for everyone.

Founded in 1993, SITE Santa Fe is a contemporary art museum. In their own words the founders are "committed to the presentation of international, contemporary arts projects on a biennial basis." SITE Santa Fe is quite unusual and very intriguing—a must-see for those who like the avant-garde.

http://www.sitesantafe.org/home1.html
(SITE Santa Fe)

FOR THE YOUNG & YOUNG AT HEART

El Rancho de las Golondrinas
334 Las Pinos Road
(505) 471-2261

Self-Guided Tours
Wednesday to Sunday, June–September, 10 A.M.–4 P.M.
Adults $5, children (ages 5–12) $2.
Seniors (62+), teens (ages 13–18), military personnel $4.
Guided tours available April–October with reservations, $5.

Festival & Theme Weekend Admission Fees
Adults $7, Children (ages 5–12) $3.
Seniors (62+), teens (ages 13–18), military personnel $5.

Wine Festival Admission Fees
21 and over $10, ages 13-20: $4.

Josefina at las Golondrinas™
All ages $20 each, all ages.
Tours open to children ages 7 through 12 and their parents.
Includes an afternoon snack and traditional craft,
as well as all-day admission to the museum.

This "ranch of the swallows" goes back to the early 1700s and used to be a stopping place on the famous Camino Real, or "Royal Road," from Mexico City to Santa Fe. Opened as a "living-history" museum in 1972, it contains restored, authentic structures erected on old foundations. In this living history museum, villagers clothed in the styles of the times show how life was lived in early New Mexico. Attractions and celebrations abound, including harvest, wine and summer festivals, sheep shearing, horsemanship and a Civil War weekend, when visitors can see the villagers involved in day-to-day aspects of these events as well as in special reenactments. The Josefina Tours include food and each child learning a traditional craft. The Museum Shop at El Rancho de las Golondrinas offers a fascinating collection of artwork and crafts in the tradition of early New Mexico. Call for information and directions from Santa Fe.

http://www.golondrinas.org/
(El Rancho de las Golondrinas)

History comes alive at El Rancho de las Golondrinas, an enthralling place to take the family. Photo © El Rancho de las Golondrinas.

Santa Fe Children's Museum

1050 Old Pecos Trail

(505) 989-8359

Open Wednesday–Saturday, 10 A.M.–5 P.M., Sunday, noon–5 P.M.

Adults & children $4, Sundays for New Mexico residents $1.

Children under 12 must be accompanied by an adult.

If you're visiting with children, especially those under 12, we have a welcome diversion for all of you. The Children's Museum is a "hands on" activity place that involves magnets, live snakes, water, bubbles you can stand inside, weaving looms, and even a climbing wall and much more. This is a respite from touring that your kids will treasure. Call for special events and times for toddlers.

http://www.santafechildrensmuseum.org/

(Santa Fe Children's Museum)

http://www.nmculture.org/

(New Mexico's Cultural Treasures site, click on index)

RESTAURANTS WITH A PAST

Rather than just recommend a restaurant for its cuisine alone, we have added a major ingredient—history—that we hope will double your dining pleasure. We've selected restaurants that not only have wonderful food but also are located in historic buildings. After all, Santa Fe is a centuries-old city, so why not pick the places that bring the romance of the ages to your experience?

http://sfWeb.ci.santa-fe.nm.us/sfpl/localhistory.html

(Santa Fe Public Library—local history)

To learn more about these restaurants, or if you wish to search Web sites for most of Santa Fe's restaurants, log on to these Web sites:

http://www.santaferestaurants.net/

(capsule descriptions of almost every restaurant in town, easy to use and very helpful)

http://www.sfol.com/restaurants/restreviews.html

(reviews of selected restaurants)

http://www.digitalcity.com/albuquerque/

(reviews of restaurants in Santa Fe and Albuquerque, including customer comments)

http://www.nmrestaurants.com/

(restaurants in New Mexico, commercial site gives restaurant discounts)

http://www.nmbars.com/

(bars in New Mexico, commercial site gives restaurant discounts)

http://999dine.com/restaurantsbycity.aspx

(restaurants in New Mexico, gives restaurant discounts)

Pricing codes used in this book

$—Inexpensive: up to $15, $$—Moderate: $15 to $30
$$$—Expensive: $30 to $50, $$$$—Very expensive: $50 or more
(Prices are for typical meal, including appetizer, side and dessert as applicable.
Prices do not include drinks, taxes or tip.)

Left: Combining casual elegance with an exquisite menu, Geronimo on Canyon Road is consistently one of Santa Fe's highest-rated restaurants.

PLAZA AREA RESTAURANTS

Anasazi Restaurant

113 Washington Avenue, Inn of the Anasazi, (505) 988-3236
Serving breakfast, lunch and dinner, $$$–$$$$

The Anasazi Restaurant, one of Santa Fe's most highly acclaimed eateries, features contemporary Southwestern cuisine, including Native American, Northern New Mexican and Southwestern. Chefs take advantage of New Mexico's abundance of fresh fruits and vegetables, as well as organic meats and poultry. The ambience is extraordinary, as the architects incorporated influences from the ancient Anasazi peoples as well as more modern arts and crafts from New Mexico's three cultures, Native American, Hispanic and Anglo.

http://www.innoftheanasazi.com/pages/restaurant.html
(Anasazi Restaurant)

http://www.guestlife.com/newmexico/dine/anasazi.html
(Anasazi Restaurant)

Bull Ring

150 Washington Avenue, (505) 983-3328
Serving lunch and dinner, $$$

Although no longer located in a 150-year-old adobe building, the Bull Ring has its own historical significance—as the most popular dining and gathering spot for state and local political figures. Primarily a steakhouse and lounge, the Bull Ring is also a place where Santa Feans know they can run into friends and share good times.

http://www.bullringsantafe.com/
(The Bull Ring)

Café Pasqual's

121 Don Gaspar Avenue, (800) 722-7672 or (505) 983-9340
Serving breakfast, lunch and dinner, $$–$$$

Although not housed in a truly historic building (circa 1920s), this venerable 24-year-old restaurant is a keeper. Always mobbed and festive, it displays murals by Oaxacan artist Leovigildo Martinez. It embodies Northern New Mexican, Old Mexican and Asian culinary traditions, served in Santa Fe style. Winner of the 1999 James Beard American Regional Cooking Classics award, Pasqual's uses use only fresh, seasonal, organic and naturally raised foods.

Note: Hours and days of operation are not included,
as these are constantly changing.

Café Pasqual's, popular with tourists and locals alike.

http://www.pasquals.com/
(Café Pasqual's)
http://www.digitalcity.com/albuquerque/entertainment/venue.adp?vid=82291
(Café Pasqual's review)

Coyote Café
132 West Water Street, (505) 983-1615
Coyote Café: serving dinner and weekend brunch, $$$$
Rooftop Cantina: serving lunch and dinner, warm months, $$–$$$
Cotton Woods: serving breakfast and lunch, $$
Mark Miller's Coyote Café is without question Santa Fe's most famous and celebrated restaurant—voted Most Popular by Zagat Guide and the winner of the James Beard Award for Best Chef of the Southwest. The dazzlingly creative blend of flavors based on the traditional cuisines of the Southwest and Latin America has now been expanded to include influences from Spain and Northern Africa. As for its location, believe it or not, this building was once the Santa Fe Bus Depot! The remodeling of this place still retains delightful touches of times gone by. For example, the serving area adjacent to the open kitchen was once the ticket counter.

http://www.coyote-cafe.com/
(Coyote Café)

Fuego at La Posada
330 East Palace Avenue, (505) 954-9670
Serving breakfast, lunch and dinner, $$$–$$$$

This warm, charming restaurant is located within the luxurious La Posada de Santa Fe, inside part of the original building erected in 1882 by Abraham Staab, one of the city's most prominent German Jewish merchants. Local folklore tells us that Julia Schuster Staab, the merchant's wife, suffered from severe post-partum depression and died in 1896. Her ghost now haunts the old part of the hotel and presents herself in the bar, in the library and on the staircase near her room. She has been known to pull covers from the bed at night in the upstairs bedroom where she died. Ask hotel personnel at the main desk to show you Julia Staab's room, No. 100—if it isn't occupied by the living!

In modern times, Fuego invites you to enjoy roaring wood fires from comfortable leather couches during the winter. In summer, listen to the whisper of the breezes on the outdoor patio. Fuego serves outstanding traditional and contemporary dishes infused with regional ingredients and flavors, often accompanied by melodic tones of a flamenco guitar.

http://www.mtn-guide.com/restad.cfm/nm102/26694.htm
(Fuego Restaurant)
http://laposada.rockresorts.com/info/din.fuego.asp
(Fuego Restaurant)
http://veronica_ceci.tripod.com/mystery/id5.html
(New Mexico mysteries)

Guadalupe Café
422 Old Santa Fe Trail, (505) 982-9762
Serving breakfast, lunch and dinner, $–$$

Guadalupe Café, an institution in Santa Fe for 29 years, is best known for its wonderful, expansive breakfast menu. Also serving lunch and dinner, the restaurant features New Mexican cooking, in portions that are ample, to say the least. Its simple adobe building, composed of several small rooms, dates to the late 1800s, when it was a private residence. After your meal, wander through the art galleries of the state Capitol, right next door.

http://www.travelbase.com/auto/article-
affiliates.cgi?name=The+Guadalupe+Cafe,+Santa+Fe&remote=linkshark
(Guadalupe Café restaurant review)
http://www.digitalcity.com/albuquerque/entertainment/venue.adp?vid=82294
(Guadalupe Café restaurant review)

Julian's

221 Shelby Street, (505) 988-2355

Serving dinner, $$$

This restaurant, on Shelby Street and close to the Plaza, has been voted Santa Fe's most romantic restaurant by both *The New Mexican* and the *Santa Fe Reporter* every year since 1998. Regional Italian dishes featuring homemade pasta are elegant yet unpretentious. As for its location, in Santa Fe terms, this lovely adobe building is not that old, only going back to the 1930s. But the feeling of the small rooms and kiva fireplaces adds an intimacy that you should experience.

http://www.juliansofsantafe.com/

(Julian's Restaurant)

http://www.digitalcity.com/albuquerque/entertainment/venue.adp?vid=180517

(Julian's review)

La Casa Sena

Sena Plaza, 125 East Palace Avenue, (505) 988-9232

Serving lunch and dinner every day, $$–$$$

Patio dining in the lovely garden courtyard of Sena Plaza.

In summer, the courtyard of La Casa Sena provides a romantic setting for drinks or a sublime dining experience. The menu features innovative Southwestern cuisine and a fabulous wine list. For a more casual dining experience, visit La Cantina, where you will be entertained by Santa Fe's only singing waiters, who perform jazz and Broadway revues nightly.

As for the location, the Sena hacienda is both charming and authentic. José Sena, a Mexican Army major, lived in this dwelling with his wife and 11 children beginning in 1831. In the original hacienda, all the windows were placed inside looking out on the inner courtyard; there weren't any outside windows then because of possible Indian attacks. Now, there are many shops and many windows! In the 1800s, the court-yard was a dusty place where livestock and chickens ran free; today, it is beautifully planted with stately old trees and seasonal flowers (see also pages 20–1).

http://www.lacasasena.com/
(La Casa Sena)
http://www.visitsantafe.com/businesspage.cfm?businessid=1947
(Sena Plaza)

La Plazuela
at La Fonda
100 East San Francisco Street, (505) 982-5511
Serving breakfast, lunch and dinner, $$–$$$

La Plazuela, a beautiful enclosed skylit courtyard restaurant in La Fonda lobby, is quite Spanish in feeling, and it's a great place to people-watch. The food, prepared by an award-winning culinary team, is Mexican and New Mexican in nature and is consistently good. Ernesto Martinez, a local artist, created the painted panes of glass depicting flowers and birds that run from the floor to the ceiling. As discussed on page 22, La Fonda itself is a much-storied place. Just being in the lobby evokes memories of times gone by. Most evenings, the area just off the bar is reserved for "Texas two-stepping."

http://www.lafondasantafe.com/food.html
(La Plazuela at La Fonda)
http://www.lafondasantafe.com/
(La Fonda)

The Old House
Located in the Eldorado Hotel
309 West San Francisco Street, (800) 286-6755 or (505) 988-4455
Serving dinner, $$$$

The Old House is the only Mobil four-star, AAA four-diamond restau-rant in the state and Zagat's top choice for New Mexico dining. Its wine list has been honored by *Wine Spectator*. The restaurant features Southwestern cuisine tempered with a touch of continental, enhanced by innovative presentation and impeccable service in a cozy, yet elegant atmosphere. As for the location, the architects tried to construct the new restaurant inside an adobe house from the late 1700s located on the hotel property. Unfortunately, it was structurally unsound and had to be

A favorite of tourists and locals alike, the Palace has long been famous for its elegance in atmosphere, menu and service.

torn down. But the Old House is on the site of the old building (and named after it), so you'll have to imagine yourself eating in a 1700s house. With the restaurant's ambience, that shouldn't be hard to do.

http://www.eldoradohotel.com/oldhouse.html

(The Old House)

Ore House on the Plaza

50 Lincoln Avenue, (505) 983-8687
Open for lunch and dinner, $$$

Located on the Plaza, the Ore House features steak, seafood and New Mexico specialties. The Cantina is open daily for drinks, appetizers and desserts. From the balcony, you can enjoy people-watching, looking out over the plaza while sipping one of 40 different margaritas. The Ore House has been winning the Wine Spectator Award of Excellence since 1993.

http://www.orehouseontheplaza.com/

(Ore House on the Plaza)

The Palace

142 West Palace Avenue, (505) 982-9891
Serving lunch and dinner, $$–$$$

It's not every day that you get the opportunity to dine in a restaurant that was once a saloon, brothel and gambling hall! The notorious (yet respected by the locals) Señora Doña Tules Barcelo ran these establishments from around 1821 to 1853. On an adjacent street, Burro Alley, the

The world-renowned Pink Adobe restaurant has been graciously
serving celebrities and locals alike for decades.

burros that carried wood from the mountains were hitched and rested
(see also page 31).

Inside the Palace, red leather booths and white linen tablecloths
remind one of colorful days gone by when "the madam" held court
here. The original building is gone, but the present one was built in the
same style. Always known for its service, this restaurant can't be beat
for a romantic evening. The Palace serves the finest continental and
Italian cuisine, including fresh seafood, homemade pastas and veal
dishes as well as fine wines.

http://www.palacerestaurant.com/
(The Palace Restaurant)

The Pink Adobe
406 Old Santa Fe Trail, (505) 983-7712
Serving lunch and dinner, $$–$$$
Café Pink, serving breakfast and lunch, $–$$

Rosalea Murphy opened this famous restaurant in 1944. It features
American/Creole and New Mexican specialties. In recent years, The
Pink Adobe has become a gathering place for locals, visitors and
famous personalities, including presidents, movie stars and some of the
most interesting characters known to Santa Fe. Its Dragon Room bar is
known the world over.

Watch the flickering candle at your table, close your eyes and for a moment you'll be transported back to the 18th century. Located in the historic Barrio de Analco neighborhood, the 300-year-old building itself was a military barracks during the Spanish occupation. The walls are three feet thick, and the restaurant is replete with fireplaces and artwork.

http://www.thepinkadobe.com
(The Pink Adobe)
http://www.santafenow.com/
(click on dining button, then on New Mexican, then Pink Adobe Web page)

The Plaza Restaurant
54 Lincoln Avenue, (505) 982-1664
Serving breakfast, lunch and dinner, $–$$

This time-honored standby—a local favorite—features some colorful neon signs and a long lunch counter along with booths against the walls and a few tables. You can depend on the place for a good Northern New Mexico meal, the basic "American" breakfast and lunch dishes, as well as Greek and international foods. As for its history, the Plaza Restaurant rates a visit because it is the oldest restaurant (1918) in town. There are others in much older buildings, but any establishment that has survived over 80 years is worth looking into. Its early-20th-century decor reflects its beginnings.

http://www.santaferestaurants.net/pages/p.html
(Santa Fe restaurants)
http://www.digitalcity.com/albuquerque/entertainment/venue.adp?vid=185231
(Plaza Restaurant review)

Rio Chama Steakhouse
414 Old Santa Fe Trail, (505) 955-0765
Serving lunch and dinner, $$$–$$$$

Rio Chama Steakhouse, located right on Old Santa Fe Trail, specializes in steak and choice beef. Although it is a new restaurant, it has the look of a venerable Pueblo Revival building and has a beautiful outdoor patio. Rio Chama Steakhouse serves the finest prime and choice dry aged steaks, chops and seafood. Located in the historic Barrio de Analco neighborhood, this building once housed another steak restaurant and before that, a private residence in the 1850s. Many of the original adobe walls were retained as the modern restaurant evolved.

http://www.riochamasteakhouse.com/
(Rio Chama Steakhouse)

Enjoy casual dining elegance at Santacafé. Brunch, lunch or dinner on the quiet outdoor patio in the summer is a special Santa Fe treat.

Rociada
304 Johnson Street, (505) 983-3800
Serving dinner, $$–$$$

The atmosphere and the food complement each other. Specializing in country-French cuisine with the most comprehensive French wine list in New Mexico, Rociada offers sophisticated fish dishes as well as steak frites and lavender crème brûlée, which reflect the eclectic style of the chef. The seasonal menu changes to offer the freshest and finest ingredients available. Patio dining is available May through October. As for the location, the building dates from 1857. Recently renovated, it reminds one of an old farmhouse set down in a trendy SoHo setting. The renovation has preserved the architectural integrity of the gracefully flowing interior with handsome turn-of-the-century tin ceilings and adobe archways.

http://www.rociada.net/site/60-SantaFe.html
(Rociada)

Santacafé
231 Washington Avenue, (505) 984-1788
Serving lunch and dinner, $$–$$$

Although the menu changes seasonally, Santacafé's American offerings are always intertwined with touches of Northern New Mexican spice. The patio opens in the late spring for outdoor dining. This elegant

The popular, family-owned restaurant The Shed celebrated its
50th anniversary on July 4, 2003.

restaurant offers artistically presented, creative dishes and a caring,
attentive staff. As for its history, Santacafé is located inside the Padre
Gallegos House, built between 1827 and 1862. Señor José M. Gallegos was a
colorful priest and a politician—quite a combination! Unfortunately, his
outspoken ways led to his being defrocked by Archbishop Lamy in 1852.
He then entered politics and was the delegate from the New Mexico
Territory from 1853 to 1855 and from 1871 to 1873. Born in 1815, he died in
1875 and is buried in Santa Fe's Rosario Cemetery.

http://www.santacafe.com/
(Santacafé)

The Shed

113½ East Palace Avenue, (505) 982-9030
Serving lunch and dinner, $–$$

Often visitors have heard about this place before they get to town—it's
been a very "Santa Fe" spot for lunch or dinner since 1953, and its chile
dishes are world-renowned. Typically Northern New Mexican, one featured dish is Blue Corn Enchiladas with red chile and garlic bread and
another is the Pollo Adobo, chicken roasted in red adobo marinade,
garlic and oregano. If you can, finish up with one of the delectable
desserts. As for the location, this historic adobe hacienda, dating to
1692, was the home of Bradford Prince, one of New Mexico's Territorial

governors. Prince purchased the home in 1879 and lived there with his wife for forty years. A room designed by Mrs. Prince in the Victorian style can be seen at the Palace of the Governors (see also page 20). The Shed also owns another restaurant, La Choza (see pages 89–90).

http://www.santaferestaurants.net/pages/s.html
(Santa Fe restaurants)

http://www.digitalcity.com/albuquerque/entertainment/venue.adp?vid=82295
(The Shed restaurant review)

Upper Crust Pizza
329 Old Santa Fe Trail
(505) 982-0000, free delivery
Serving lunch and dinner, $

This pizza restaurant, consistently voted "Best of Santa Fe," has been around since 1979. In addition to the traditional pizzas, Upper Crust creates some in Santa Fe style with green chile or Mexican sausage, with whole-wheat or traditional Italian crusts. It also serves great sandwiches, calzones and salads. You can enjoy the Santa Fe scene from the large front patio, or, if you prefer, you can have your pizza delivered to your room. Strange place for a pizza parlor to be, but this building is part of the Barrio de Analco. The back dining room is actually a part of the oldest house in Santa Fe (see page 26).

http://www.uppercrustpizza.com/
(Upper Crust Pizza)

CANYON ROAD

The Compound
653 Canyon Road, (505) 982-4353
Serving lunch and dinner, $$$$

If the weather is warm and sunny (your chances are very good), opt for lunch or dinner on the garden patio. Contemporary American food reigns here, and it is excellent, paired with a thoughtful selection of wine and classical service in a relaxed atmosphere. Attention to detail and professional service complement the dining experience. As for the location, this house was built around 1850 with small dining rooms that spill out onto the gorgeous enclosed patio. Before its incarnation as a restaurant, The Compound was the centerpiece of a group of houses on Canyon Road known as the McComb Compound. In the earlier

El Farol offers an unbeatable mix—an elegant restaurant featuring genuine Spanish ambience—and one of the hottest night spots in town.

part of the 20th century, when Santa Fe was a long way from the rest of the world, movie stars, industrialists and socialites visited, where they could rent a house in relative seclusion. Alexander Girard, whose collections of folk art grace the Museum of International Folk Art, decorated the original restaurant. Some of his touches are still to be seen in the updated Compound.

http://www.compoundrestaurant.com/
(*The Compound*)

http://www.braniffinternational.org/people/alexandergirard.htm
(*Alexander Girard*)

El Farol

808 Canyon Road, (505) 983-9912
Serving lunch and dinner, $$–$$$

Santa Fe's oldest restaurant and cantina, El Farol is a local favorite for both its excellent food and superb entertainment. The restaurant serves award-winning traditional and contemporary Spanish cuisine, featuring over 35 different *tapas*—small, delectable Spanish dishes or appetizers. You can mix or match these delectable treats to create a meal or order a more traditional dinner. The famous and infamous can show up here—good people-watching! Owner David Salazar invites you to come and enjoy the finest live entertainment in Santa Fe, including jazz, soul, folk, R&B and flamenco, every night of the week.

As for its location, El Farol is housed in an adobe building that has served artists, locals and stray bohemians since 1835. If they could talk, these thick old walls would tell stories of lovers, poets, musicians and artists, like painter Alfred Morang, whose frescoes adorn them. These were painted between 1945 and 1952, when the cantina still had dirt floors. The decor is a cross between rustic Spanish and rustic Santa Fe.

http://elfarolsf.com/
(El Farol)

Geronimo
724 Canyon Road, (505) 982-1500
Serving lunch and dinner, $$–$$$

After 10 celebrated years, Geronimo has established a reputation as the place to dine in Santa Fe. Owners Cliff Skoglund and Chris Harvey have succeeded in bringing unparalleled sophistication with a romantic, elegant atmosphere, creating a fabulous backdrop for the Global Fusion-Southwest-influenced creations. Appetizers, salads and desserts along with seafood and meat dishes alike are wonderfully prepared in this romantic spot. The building is over 250 years old, and the interior is reflective of that period in a sparse, elegant way. This 1756 landmark adobe was built by Geronimo Lopez (see also page 58).

http://www.guestlife.com/newmexico/dine/geronimo.html
(Geronimo Restaurant)
http://www.epicurious.com/erg/santafe/geronimo.html
(Epicurious *review*)

GUADALUPE DISTRICT & AGUA FRÍA STREET

Café San Estevan
428 Agua Fría Street, (505) 995-1996
Serving breakfast, lunch and dinner, $$

A feeling of old Mexico pervades this lovely old adobe, with its indirect lighting, glowing fireplaces and Hispanic folk art. In the summer, food is served on the *portal*. The attentive waitstaff serves dishes ranging from typical to rather eclectic Northern New Mexican fare, with a "soupcon" of French. It prides itself on using all organic products,

The ambience and authentic cuisine of Old Mexico set El Encanto apart.

including food from local farmers. Located just off Guadalupe Street, the building housing Café San Estevan dates back to the 1800s. It's representative of many the older buildings that line Agua Fría.

http://www.concierge.com/travelideas/food/bestrestaurants/index.ssf?cafesanestevan

(Café San Estevan)

El Encanto
416 Agua Fría Street, (505) 988-5991
Serving lunch and dinner, $$–$$$

This building has housed a restaurant for many years, El Encanto being the latest. Specializing in authentic Mexican cuisine, El Encanto provides a setting and food that will transport you to Old Mexico. Enjoy outdoor dining in summer. This structure was once a Dominican convent right across the street from the Santuario de Guadalupe, a late-18th-century church. The old, thick adobe walls wouldn't talk much even if they could, but they would share with you a sense of the quiet that once prevailed.

http://www.santaferestaurants.net/pages/e.html

(Santa Fe restaurant guide)

Ristra

548 Agua Fría Street, (505) 982-8608
Serving dinner, $$$

Ristra offers an eclectic blend of Southwestern and French cuisine. The intimate surroundings are warm and casual, yet elegant. Weather permitting, you can dine on the lovely outdoor patio. As for its location, this building is unlike most of the classic adobe and Territorial buildings that make up much of Santa Fe. It's an old bungalow-style cottage, probably built after 1880 when the railroad came through and bricks became more plentiful. As you walk through the small dining room areas, however, the interior has an indigenous adobe feel.

http://www.ristrarestaurant.com/
(Ristra)

Tomasita's Santa Fe Station

500 South Guadalupe Street, (505) 983-5721
Serving lunch and dinner daily, $–$$

Always a popular place because of its Northern New Mexican cooking and its moderate prices, Tomasita's is always crowded. No reservations are accepted, so be prepared to wait—but you can get a drink from the bar and the wait is worth it! The frozen margaritas are a hallmark of the restaurant, as are such dishes as chile rellenos and blue-corn chicken enchiladas. The building once housed a brick trackside warehouse for the "Chile Line," a spur railroad that ran from 1884 to 1941. In its day, it was the "lifeline" to Northern New Mexico towns and pueblos.

http://www.digitalcity.com/albuquerque/dining/venue.adp?vid=197765
(Tomasita's Santa Fe Station)

SANTA FE'S BEST-KEPT SECRETS

The following restaurants are favorites with locals and always packed. Most do not take reservations, but all are worth the wait. They are in general more casual and less expensive.

Blue Corn Café

133 Water Street, (just off the Plaza), (505) 984-1800
4056 Cerrillos Road, (near Villa Linda Mall), (505) 438-1800
Serving lunch and dinner, $–$$

Enjoy locally brewed beer and ale along with a variety of Northern New Mexico specialties.

http://www.bluecorncafe.com/
(Blue Corn Café)

Bobcat Bite

420 Old Las Vegas Highway, (505) 983-5319, call for directions
Serving lunch and dinner Wednesday through Saturday, $
Known all over for its green chile cheeseburgers.

http://www.digitalcity.com/albuquerque/dining/venue.adp?vid=82296
(review of Bobcat Bite)

Cloud Cliff Bakery Café Artspace

1805 Second Street, (505) 983-6254
Serving breakfast and lunch, $–$$
The Cloud Cliff menu is eclectic, organic, nourishing and thoughtful,
featuring homemade bread and pastries, sandwiches and soups.

http://www.kanseki.net/cloudcliff/index.shtml
(Cloud Cliff Café)

Cowgirl Bar B Q & Western Grill

319 South Guadalupe St., (505) 982-2565
Serving lunch and dinner, with Saturday and Sunday breakfasts, $–$$
Specializing in mesquite-smoked pit barbecue as well as steak, chicken
and New Mexican favorites with nightly live entertainment.

http://www.cowgirl-santafe.com/
(Cowgirl)

Harry's Roadhouse

96-B Old Las Vegas Highway, (505) 989-4629
Serving breakfast, lunch and dinner, $–$$
A local favorite, Harry's menu features a wide variety of foods with
something to please any taste, all of it fresh and homemade.

http://www.santaferestaurants.net/pages/h.html
(Harry's Roadhouse)

La Choza

905 Alarid Street, (505) 982-0909
Serves lunch and dinner, $–$$
Specializing in Northern New Mexican food since 1984, La Choza is situated in an old adobe that served as the ranch house and bunk house
for the Mercer Ranch in the early 1900s. Owned and operated by The
Shed Restaurant (see page 83), La Choza is a favorite with locals who
come to savor the sopaipillas, chalupas, tamales and carne adovada.

http://www.santaferestaurants.net/pages/l.html
(La Choza Restaurant)
http://www.frommers.com/destinations/moredining.cfm?h_id=9294
(La Choza Restaurant review)

Maria's New Mexican Kitchen
555 West Cordova Road, (505) 983-7929
Serving lunch and dinner, $–$$

Maria's is known for margaritas—over 100 are featured—as well as for its fajitas. Enjoy patio dining in the summer. The owner, Al Lucero, is the author of *The Great Margarita Book*.

http://www.marias-santafe.com/
(Maria's New Mexican Kitchen)
http://www.booksupermart.com/
(to order The Great Margarita Book*)*

Pranzo Italian Grill
540 Montezuma Avenue, (505) 984-2645
Serving lunch and dinner, $$

Voted best Italian restaurant by locals year after year, Pranzo offers fresh pasta, fresh fish and grilled meats. Reservations recommended.

http://www.santaferestaurants.net/pages/p.html
(Pranzo Italian Grill)
http://www.digitalcity.com/albuquerque/entertainment/venue.adp?vid=180495
(review of Pranzo Italian Grill)

Santa Fe Baking Co. & Café
504 West Cordova Road, (505) 988-4292
Serving breakfast and lunch, $

One of the area's favorite meeting places, especially for breakfast, coffee break and lunch. Bakery as well as full breakfast and lunch menus.

http://www.santafebaking.com/
(Santa Fe Baking Co. & Café)

Second Street Brewery
1814 Second Street, (505) 982-3030
Serving appetizers, lunch and dinner, $–$$

A neighborhood brewpub offering locally made English-style ales and authentic international pub food, frequently with live music.

http://www.secondstreetbrewery.com/
(Second Street Brewery)

Steaksmith
104-B Old Las Vegas Highway, (505) 988-3333
Serving dinner, $$–$$$
Santa Fe's steak and seafood house since 1973 features choice aged beef
as well as an extensive appetizer and light meal menu in the lounge.
http://www.santafesteaksmith.com/
(Steaksmith)

Tecolote Café
1203 Cerrillos Road, (505) 988-1362
Serving breakfast and lunch until 2 p.m., $
Tourists and locals alike agree that this is the place to go for a great
homemade breakfast. Large portions, lots of chile and friendly service.
http://www.visitsantafe.com/businesspage.cfm?businessid=1153
(Tecolote Café)
http://chefmoz.org/United_States/NM/Santa_Fe/Tecolote_Cafe957148904.html
(review of Tecolote Café)

Tesuque Village Market
Five miles north of Santa Fe in Tesuque, (505) 988-8848. call for directions
Serving breakfast, lunch and dinner, $–$$
Enjoy American and Southwestern specialties. Also sells groceries, pas-
tries, deli items and liquor.
http://www.frommers.com/destinations/moredining.cfm?h_id=9305
(Tesuque Village Market)

Tia Sophia's
210 West San Francisco Street, (505) 983-9880
Serving breakfast and lunch, $
This popular downtown restaurant is famous for its breakfast burritos.
The menu has the following note: "Not responsible for too hot chile."
http://www.santaferestaurants.net/pages/t.html
(Tia Sophia's)

Zia Diner
326 South Guadalupe, (505) 988-7008
Serving lunch and dinner, $–$$
This upscale diner features daily specials of pasta, fish, chicken and
diner comfort food.
http://www.santaferestaurants.net/pages/z.html
(Zia Diner)

LODGINGS WITH A PAST

Whenever I visit a historical town I want to feel its history and the romance, so I search for accommodations that go hand in glove with the roots of the place. Here is a list of Santa Fe lodgings for historical bedding-down. There are, of course, motels galore on Cerrillos Road and several beautiful but new upscale hotels in town, and you're welcome to check these out (see pages 102–5 for more information), but I recommend you go for the history and the homemade breakfasts.

Pricing codes used in this book

Room rates change from season to season and even from week to week. This is only meant to be a general guide; call for exact rates.

Category	Cost
$$	$65–$100
$$$	$100–$150
$$$$	Over $150

HISTORIC BED & BREAKFASTS

Adobe Abode Bed & Breakfast
202 Chapelle Street, (505) 983-3133, $$$

Located close to the Plaza, this 1907 adobe has rooms that reflect different styles and moods—Provence, perhaps, or Cowboy, or Mexican. Along with its Old World charm come amenities such as cushy robes and designer linens, along with cookies and sherry served all day.

http://www.adobeabode.com/

(Adobe Abode Bed and Breakfast)

Left: La Posada de Santa Fe Resort and Spa features a quiet elegance. Even if you do not stay here, you should drop by to enjoy your favorite beverage in one of its peaceful sitting rooms.

Alexander's Inn

529 East Palace Avenue, (888) 321-5123 or (505) 986-1431, $$–$$$
This 1903 Craftsman-style house is yet another architectural gem in the
land of adobe homes. It sits several blocks from the Plaza on esteemed
Palace Avenue. The rooms have a country feel; the deck and garden are
lovely. Breakfasts are continental—and excellent.

http://www.alexanders-inn.com/
(Alexander's Inn)

Don Gaspar Inn

623 Don Gaspar Avenue, (888) 986-8664 or (505) 986-8664, $$$
Located in a historic neighborhood where many of the early merchants
built their homes, this inn compound features three older buildings: a
1900–1910 arts-and-crafts brick bungalow, a 1910 Territorial building
and a 1930s Pueblo-style building. All three have a Victorian interior-
decorating theme. The ultimate garden features irises and lilies and
more in a fountain setting that one would expect to see on the East
Coast. Voted one of the Top Ten Romantic Inns in the Country for
2003 by *American Historic Inns.*

http://www.dongaspar.com/
(Don Gaspar Inn)

El Paradero Bed and Breakfast Inn

220 West Manhattan Avenue, (505) 988-1177, $$
Originally a Spanish farmhouse built between 1800 and 1820, this build-
ing was once far from "town." Now it's near the Sanbusco Market
Center, the Farmers' Market and many restaurants. Pillars were added
in the late 19th century, Victorian touches in 1912. Its current owners
tried to keep the "adobe farmhouse feeling" intact, and they have succeeded. Some rooms are moderately priced; the more expensive ones
have different furnishings and mountain views. Breakfasts are ample
and feature a special entrée daily.

http://www.elparadero.com/
(El Paradero Bed and Breakfast Inn)

Four Kachinas Inn

512 Webber Street, (800) 397-2564 or (505) 982-2550, $$$
Located on a quiet residential street in the Don Gaspar Historic District,
the Four Kachinas Inn is a short block from the Plaza. One of the guest
rooms is located in the historic Digneo House, built in 1910 by Carlo

Breakfast at the Grant Corner Inn is so delightful that it draws
many people who are not guests.

Digneo, one of the Italian stone masons who completed the St. Francis
Cathedral for Archbishop Lamy in the late 19th century. All the rooms
feature quality Southwestern art and locally made crafts. In summer
enjoy a delightful continental breakfast in the outside garden patio.

http://www.fourkachinas.com/

(Four Kachinas Inn)

Grant Corner Inn

122 Grant Avenue, (800) 964-9003 or (505) 983-6678, $$–$$$
This lovely inn was not done in the usual Santa Fe architecture styles of
Pueblo Revival or Territorial, but rather in the Colonial Manor style
(circa 1906). Some who built houses in that era came from the Midwest
or the East and wanted to construct the type of house to which they
were accustomed—hence the Grant Corner Inn. With its weeping willow tree, wraparound porch and white picket fence, it is quintessential
Victorian. It is also just steps from The Georgia O'Keeffe Museum.

The inn has 10 rooms, each filled with antiques including quilts and
photography. Its best feature is breakfast, served to guests and the public
as well. Spectacular entrées include French toast, blintzes and burritos.
Tasty muffins, breads and cookies are created on the premises.

http://www.grantcornerinn.com/

(Grant Corner Inn)

Guadalupe Inn

604 Agua Fría Street, (505) 989-7422, $$$

Enjoy traditional Santa Fe family hospitality in this small inn, a "truly Santa Fe" experience. Owned and operated by three members of the Quintana family, the inn was built on the site of their grandfather's store on Agua Fría, very close to the historic Santuario de Guadalupe (see page 65). Although the building itself is quite new, the land has been in the Quintana family for generations; in fact, Concha S. Quintana, now in her 90s, will regale you at breakfast with tale after tale of Santa Fe in the old days, when she used to work at La Fonda and met all the artists and celebrities. Some rooms have whirlpool tubs, fireplaces and mountain views. For breakfast, visitors select from a menu ranging from traditional family New Mexico favorites to eggs any style and pancakes.

http://www.guadalupeinn.com/
(Guadalupe Inn)
http://www.thesantafesite.com/MiniWeb/GuadalupeInn.html
(Guadalupe Inn)

Hacienda Nicholas

320 East Marcy Street, (888) 321-5123 or (505) 986-1431, $$$–$$$$

Carolyn Lee, owner of both Alexander's Inn and The Madeleine, recently added another historic inn to her B&B "empire." The Hacienda Nicholas, named for her son (the other inns are also named for her children) is a beautifully understated adobe. In her words: "The decor throughout the house is an elegant blend of Southwest meets Provence." Legend has it that this beautiful adobe hacienda was built in 1910 by Antonio Abelard Rodriguez for his bride, the exquisite Doña Isabella. Breakfasts are substantial and include such entrées as blueberry pancakes, quiche and breakfast frittatas.

http://www.haciendanicholas.com/
(Hacienda Nicholas)

Inn of the Five Graces

(Formerly Seret's 1001 Nights)

150 East De Vargas Street, (866) 507-1001 or (505) 992-0957, $$$$

Inn of the Five Graces is located in the Barrio de Analco (see pages 26–8). The inkeepers have chosen to combine Santa Fe's Southwestern buildings with an alluring amalgamation of textiles and wooden pieces from Turkey, India, Tibet and Afghanistan, with a warm, romantic result. The years of construction of the buildings themselves ranges from 1888 to 1950. New Mexico river rock was used for one built in 1938. Recently acquired by the Garrett Hotel Group, Inn of the Five Graces is high on service and amenities. All units come with kitchens and elegant baths, and many have fireplaces.

http://www.fivegraces.com/
(Inn of the Five Graces)

Inn of the Turquoise Bear

342 Buena Vista Street, (800) 396-4104 or (505) 983-0798, $$$–$$$$
This B&B dates to the mid-1800s and was once the home of poet Witter Bynner (1881–1968), a noted member of the cultural group flourishing at that time in Santa Fe. The bedrooms are simple but well appointed with flowers, fruits and complimentary robes; the public rooms are ranch-like and very appealing.

The inn's sense of history lies partly in who "partied" here. Mr. Bynner hosted many bashes with such notables as D.H. Lawrence, Ansel Adams, Igor Stravinsky, Willa Cather, Georgia O'Keeffe, Edna St. Vincent Millay, Robert Frost, Martha Graham, Rita Hayworth and Frida Kahlo. Oh, to be a fly on the wall at those soirées!

http://elibrary.unm.edu/oanm/NmLcU/nmlcu1%23ms186/nmlcu1%23ms186_m6.html
(Witter Bynner bio outline)
http://www.turquoisebear.com/
(Inn of the Turquoise Bear)

La Tienda Inn & Duran House

445–447 & 511 West San Francisco Street,
(800) 889-7611 or (505) 989-8259, $$$
The innkeepers took an old local grocery store and small adjoining apartment building and transformed them into an elegant inn. The renovation of the store and the century-old Territorial-style house next door (now listed on the state Historical Register) earned an award from the city of Santa Fe. Only four blocks from the center of town, it has kept its charm of a simpler era. Rooms are individually furnished with antiques, Spanish and Native American artifacts, and beautiful hand-crafted furniture. A delicious selection of warm breads, fresh fruit, cereal, yogurt and juices is served each morning in guests' rooms or in the courtyard and gardens.

http://www.latiendabb.com/
(La Tienda Inn and Duran House)

The Madeleine

106 Faithway Street, (888) 321-5123 or (505) 986-1431, $$–$$$
The doyenne of Alexander's Inn, Carolyn Lee, also owns this unusual, circa-1886 three-story Queen Anne house exemplifying the décor and decorations of the period. It's on the same street as one of the oldest Episcopal churches (Church of the Holy Faith) in Santa Fe. Enjoy The Madeleine's offerings of delectable baked goods and tasty, ample breakfasts.

http://www.madeleineinn.com/
(The Madeleine)

Pueblo Bonito Inn

138 West Manhattan Avenue, (800) 461-4599 or (505) 984-8001, $$$
Built in 1873, this old adobe edifice is but a short walk to the Plaza. Most of the furnishings are Southwestern—*santos*, paintings and pottery—and kiva fireplaces grace every one of the 15 rooms. A continental breakfast is served buffet style; later in the day, relax with afternoon tea.

http://www.pueblobonitoinn.com/
(Pueblo Bonito Inn)

Territorial Inn

215 Washington Avenue, (866) 230-7737 or (505) 989-7737, $$$
The Territorial Inn is an 1896 Victorian edifice right in the middle of town—walk a mere two blocks down Washington Avenue and you're at the Plaza. Two of the 10 guestrooms have fireplaces, eight have private baths and all are elegantly furnished. In the morning, enjoy an expanded continental breakfast; at mid-afternoon, savor fresh cookies and coffee; and in the evening, relax with brandy and chocolates.

The 15-room Marcy wing adjacent to the main house was completed in July 2001. A beautifully decorated "breakfast court" is the centerpiece of this wing, which features spacious, well-appointed rooms as well as one- and two-bedroom suites.

http://www.territorialinn.com/
(Territorial Inn)

HISTORIC HOTELS

The entrance and patio of the Hotel St. Francis.

The Hotel St. Francis

210 Don Gaspar Avenue, (800) 529-5700 or 983-5700, $$$$

The Hotel St. Francis—listed in the National Register of Historic Places—is close to the Plaza, shopping and wonderful restaurants. Guest quarters embody a Victorian sensibility, with brass and iron beds and furniture of cherry wood and marble. The hotel's formal afternoon tea with scones and finger sandwiches is a splendid daily ritual. (For its history, see page 28.)

http://www.hotelstfrancis.com/

(Hotel St. Francis)

La Fonda

100 East San Francisco Street, (800) 523-5002 or (505) 982-5511, $$$$

The oldest hotel site in town, La Fonda features hand-painted furniture, beamed ceilings and wrought-iron light fixtures in each of its 167 rooms. In 1998, La Fonda completed La Terraza, a rooftop garden featuring 14 private luxury rooms and suites. The lobby is bustling all day

You step back into Santa Fe's past when you enter the lobby of La Fonda.

long, and the bar is filled with music every night. La Fonda is truly a
terrific Santa Fe experience. (For its history, see page 22.)

http://www.lafondasantafe.com/
(La Fonda)

La Posada de Santa Fe Resort and Spa

330 East Palace Avenue, (800) 727-5276 or (505) 986-0000, $$$$
La Posada is one of Santa Fe's loveliest hotels. Built around the Staab
mansion (1870s), the hotel is located on six prime acres of land only a
few blocks from the Plaza. Now encompassing 159 rooms with kiva fireplaces and patios, it is a true oasis right in the center of town. La
Posada spa, Avanyu, is noted in the chapter on shopping and spas, page
124. To learn more about one of its spooky inhabitants (and one of
Santa Fe's most famous ghosts) see page 76.

http://www.laposadadesantafe.com/
(La Posada)
http://laposada.rockresorts.com/info/spa.asp
(Avanyu Spa)

HISTORIC AND OUT OF TOWN

The entrance to Bishop's Lodge.

Bishop's Lodge

Bishop's Lodge Road (10 minutes from downtown, call for directions)
(800) 732-2240 or (505) 983-6377, $$$$

Secluded in its own private valley in the foothills of the Sangre de
Cristo Mountains, this exquisite hideaway has been ranked by *Travel &
Leisure* as one of America's top 100 hotels and resorts, as well as by
Conde Nast Traveler as one of the 500 best places to stay in the whole
world. Established in 1851 as a retreat for Jean Baptiste Lamy, Bishop's
Lodge has become New Mexico's vacation playground. In addition to
luxurious accommodations, the resort offers lush gardens, fishing, hiking, tennis courts, horseback riding, swimming pool, fabulous spa,
wellness center, and nearby golf and skiing. Add to all this a fabulous
restaurant and you have a vacation destination that would be hard to
beat anywhere!

http://www.bishopslodge.com/

(Bishop's Lodge)

Sunrise Springs Inn & Retreat

242 Los Pinos Road (about 20 minutes from downtown, call for directions)
(800) 955-0028 or (505) 471-3600, $$$

This retreat is not historical, but its uniqueness suggests its inclusion in this book. Overnight guests enjoy accommodations to enhance the spirit, including outdoor hot tubs, Japanese tea, massage/wellness services and spa, sweat lodge, raku pottery-making, wondrous gardens, ceremonial circles, pathways for exercise and meditation, and all-natural cooking choices at the Blue Heron Restaurant (see also page 126).

http://www.sunrisesprings.com/
(Sunrise Springs)

OTHER WELL-KNOWN HOTELS

Santa Fe, being famous for its hospitality as well as its history, also boasts some world-class hotels of recent origin. In spite of being relatively new, these hotels manage to create the ambience of Old Santa Fe as well as— and in some cases better than—the older places. Several of these newer hotels are world-renowned and need to be included in this book.

Eldorado Hotel

309 West San Francisco Street, (800) 286-6755 or (505) 988-4455, $$$$

Santa Fe's first AAA four-diamond, four-star hotel is located next to the Plaza. This upscale hotel features rooms with fireplaces and mountain views as well as two restaurants, the critically acclaimed Old House (see page 78) and the Eldorado Court and Lounge.

http://www.eldoradohotel.com/
(Eldorado Hotel)
http://www.eldoradohotel.com/cgi-bin/specials.cgi
(Internet specials on room rates)

Hilton of Santa Fe

100 Sandoval Street, (800) 336-3676 or (505) 988-2811, $$$-$$$$

Decorated throughout with beautiful regional artwork and antiquities, the Hilton of Santa Fe also preserves the historic Ortiz Hacienda, built in the 17th century and one of Santa Fe's well known historical sites. For restaurants, you can select from the Piñon Grill, El Cañon, and the Chamisa Courtyard Café.

http://www.hiltonofsantafe.com/
(Hilton of Santa Fe)
http://www.hiltonofsantafe.com/roomspecials.cgi
(Internet specials)

Hotel Plaza Real

125 Washington Avenue, (877) 901-ROOM or (505) 988-4900, $$$$
Minutes from the Plaza, Hotel Plaza Real is a picturesque boutique
hotel featuring wood-burning fireplaces and handcrafted furniture and
art. The hotel also is home to Jesse's Wood-Fired Pizza and Spirits and,
in the summer, an outdoor fajita grill.

http://www.buynewmexico.com/heritagehotels/plaza_real/plaza_real_home.html
(Hotel Plaza Real)

Hotel Santa Fe

1501 Paseo de Peralta, (800) 825-9876 or (505) 982-1200, $$$$
Owned by Picuris Pueblo (see page 172), Santa Fe's only Native American-
owned hotel offers both comfort and culture. The hotel sits just off the
Plaza and occupies three acres adorned by Native American sculpture and
totems, wildflowers and privacy. Its restaurant, Amaya, features Native
foods and, when weather permits, Indian dancing outdoors on the patio.

http://www.hotelsantafe.com/
(Hotel Santa Fe)
http://www.hotelsantafe.com/hot.htm
(Internet specials on room rates)

Inn at Loretto

211 Old Santa Fe Trail, (800) 727-5531 or (505) 988-5531, $$$$
Situated next to the historic Loretto Chapel (see page 24), the Inn at
Loretto features interior wall murals, carved ceilings, and door frames
that incorporate designs, petroglyphs and weavings found in Pueblo
and Spanish artistry. The hotel's fine-dining restaurant serves breakfast,
lunch and dinner. In 2002 the hotel opened SpaTerre, offering unique
spa treatments as well as the usual spa amenities.

http://www.hotelloretto.com/
(Inn at Loretto)

Inn of the Anasazi

113 Washington Avenue, (800) 688-8100 or (505) 988-3030, $$$$
A four-diamond, four-star hotel, the Inn of the Anasazi was designed as
an artful blend of Southwestern culture and luxurious amenities.
Handcrafted furnishings, four–poster beds and gas-lit fireplaces are
framed under traditional ceilings of vigas and latillas. Located steps
from the Plaza, the hotel also boasts one of Santa Fe's most highly rated
restaurants (see page 74).

http://www.innoftheanasazi.com/
(Inn of the Anasazi)

Inn of the Governors

101 West Alameda Street, (800) 234-4534 or (505) 982-4333, $$$-$$$$
Located just off the Plaza, Inn of the Governors features rooms with
special touches such as Mexican folk art, kiva fireplaces, colorful
painted lamps, handcrafted desks, trunks and armoires. This hotel fea-
tures a complimentary full breakfast and the Del Charro Saloon, which
offers light foods and desserts.

http://www.innofthegovernors.com/
(Inn of the Governors)

OTHER PLACES TO STAY

As mentioned at the beginning of this chapter, there are many other
places to stay in Santa Fe, places that may suit your needs just fine, even
though they may lack the historical sensibilities of those listed above.
Santa Fe has most of the big hotel chains as well as many smaller inde-
pendent motels, mainly located along Cerrillos Road. Besides the usual
sources such as AAA, travel brochures, membership plans or credit-
card promotions, you can find many places to stay (and restaurants,
attractions and events as well) on the following Web sites:

Noncommercial sites

You can make reservations at almost any lodging establishment from
these sites. They contain no commercial messages.

http://www.santafe.org/
*(official Santa Fe site for visitors, noncommercial—businesses do not pay for their
listings, very complete, links to Web sites, includes descriptions of places)*

http://www.sfdetours.com/accommodations/
*(Santa Fe Detours reservation service, all lodgings, reservations by phone
or e-mail—select your accommodation by price, etc.)*

Membership or group sites

You either need to be a member and use a password to enter site, or
listings include only that site's own members, or managed properties:

http://www.aaa-newmexico.com/travel/
(AAA reservations statewide, for AAA members nationwide)

http://www.nmhotels.com/
*(New Mexico Lodging Association site, reservations statewide,
listings are members of NMLA, commercial)*

http://santafe.net/casas/

(Casas de Santa Fe, rental of furnished homes by night or week)

Commercial sites

Lodging establishments pay to be listed on these sites, and some have other commercial messages.

http://www.santafe.worldWeb.com/

(Santa Fe Tourism World Wide Web travel guide, commercial)

http://www.santafescene.com/

(Santa Fe Scene online tourist guide, commercial, includes virtual walking tour and train info)

http://santafestation.com/

(Includes dining guide and calendars of events, commercial)

http://www.nmtravel.com/

(Hotel and lodging reservations for whole state of New Mexico, certain lodgings only, commercial)

http://santafehotels.com/

(Santa Fe Accommodations, certain lodgings only, commercial, includes Web cam)

http://www.santafecentralres.com/

(Santa Fe Central Reservations, gives 800 number, no reservations on line, certain lodgings only, commercial)

http://www.santafe.com/

(Santa Fe On Line Magazine, listings and reviews of accommodations and restaurants with addresses and phone numbers, also attractions and the arts, commercial)

http://www.visitsantafe.com/

(listings and links for accommodations and restaurants, sorted by type, also activities, the arts and maps)

http://www.thesantafesite.com/

(listings and some links for accommodations and restaurants, events and outdoor activities, also some features relating to Santa Fe subjects)

http://www.santafeinformation.com/

(similar to other general information sites above, but includes a Web cam)

http://www.sfaol.com/

(similar to above sites, contains a wider variety of links)

GALLERIES, SHOPPING & SPAS

We have observed that shopping in Santa Fe is a way of life for most visitors! And, we know that at the end of a shopping day, a person may well long for a whirlpool, a swim or a deep massage. After such pampering, one should be ready for yet another day of shopping, sightseeing and gallery hopping.

Our "shopping list" takes in an array of places we think you will enjoy. The list includes art and photography galleries, shops and museums offering Native American art and antiquities, stores that specialize in Western furniture and Western wear, and museums and bookstores where you'll find volumes on the Southwest.

Put on your walking shoes, because most of these places can be reached on foot from your lodgings. These are just some of the many wonderful shops located all over Santa Fe. Check the Yellow Pages of the telephone book for a full list.

Before heading out to the galleries, you might like to visit them on line. You can do so with the help of this book and by using the following site:

http://www.collectorsguide.com/

(Collectors Guide, arts magazine covering Albuquerque, Santa Fe and Taos, features extensive links to gallery sites)

Left: When browsing around downtown, you combine shopping with historical sightseeing..

GALLERIES

The Gerald Peters Gallery features one of the city's finest art collections.

Two of Santa Fe's Oldest & Finest Collections of Art

Gerald Peters Gallery
1011 Paseo de Peralta
(505) 954-5700

For over 25 years, the Gerald Peters Gallery has been showing museum-quality art and sculpture. Located in a new building designed in the adobe Pueblo Revival style, the gallery takes you on a perfectly splendid stylistic tour in its 8,500 feet of exhibition space. In the centerpiece gallery are works by Taos Society of Artists and the Santa Fe Colony. Other galleries display 20th-century European and American modernists, wildlife art and photography. It's easy to spend time here; take a moment to peruse the in-depth art bookstore as well. The outdoor sculpture garden features a lovely lawn, fine stonework, a beautiful waterfall and an ever-changing array of outdoor sculpture.

http://www.gpgallery.com/
(Gerald Peters Gallery)

Nedra Matteucci Galleries
1075 Paseo de Peralta
(505) 982-4631

In the 1900s, this gallery was a farm situated along a dusty road. It was expanded over a period of time to become an art gallery owned by the painter Nicolas Wolashuk. In 1972, the property was sold to Rex Arrowsmith and Forrest Fenn and was turned into the beautiful gallery it is today. Arrowsmith and Fenn specialized in the Taos Society of Artists; Western collectibles were and are featured today.

In 1988 the gallery was sold to Nedra Matteucci, who introduced contemporary painters into the mix. She expanded the beautiful (some say, the most beautiful) outdoor sculpture garden. Sculptures by Doug Hyde, Don Ostermiller and Glenna Goodacre may be enjoyed in this pastoral setting featuring a large, romantic pond, verdant trees and a softly running waterfall. Associated with this gallery and showing contemporary art from around the country is Nedra Matteucci Fine Art on Canyon Road (below).

http://www.matteucci.com/

(Nedra Matteucci Galleries)

Venerable Art Galleries of Canyon Road

Allene Lapides Gallery
558 Canyon Road, (505) 984-0191
http://www.lapidesgallery.com/

Altermann Galleries
203 Canyon Road, (505) 820-1644
225 Canyon Road, (505) 983-1590
http://www.altermann.com/

Canfield Gallery
414 Canyon Road, (505) 988-4199
(carries American Indian antiquities as well)
http://www.canfieldgallery.com/

The Munson Gallery
225 Canyon Road, (505) 983-1657
http://www.munsongallery.com/

Nedra Matteucci Fine Art
555 Canyon Road, (505) 983-2731
http://www.nedramatteuccifineart.com/

Ventana Fine Art
400 Canyon Road, (505) 983-8815
http://www.ventanafineart.com/

Zaplin-Lampert Gallery
651 Canyon Road, (505) 982-6100
http://www.zaplinlampert.com/

Other Fine Santa Fe Galleries

Chiaroscuro Gallery
439 Camino Del Monte Sol, (505) 992-0711
708 Canyon Road, (505) 986-9197
http://www.chiaroscurosantafe.com/

Cline Fine Art
135 West Palace Avenue, (505) 982-5328
http://www.clinefineart.com/

Davis Mather Folk Art Gallery
141 Lincoln Avenue, (505) 983-1660
http://www.visitsantafe.com/category.cfm?categoryid=1533

Lewallen Contemporary
129 West Palace Avenue, (505) 988-8997
http://www.lewallenart.com/

Owings Dewey Fine Art
76 East San Francisco Street, (505) 982-6244
Owings Dewey North, 120 East Marcy Street, (505) 986-9088
http://www.owingsdewey.com/

Peyton-Wright
237 East Palace Avenue, (505) 999-9888
http://www.peytonwright.com/

Price-Dewey Galleries
53 Old Santa Fe Trail, (505) 982-8632
http://www.deweyltd.com/

Riva Yares Gallery
123 Grant Avenue, (505) 984-0330
http://www.rivayaresgallery.com/

Out of Town, but Worth a Visit

The outdoor sculpture garden at Shidoni is one of the most unique anywhere.

Shidoni
Foundry, Sculpture Gallery and Gardens
Bishop's Lodge Road, close to the village of Tesuque, (505) 988-8001
www.shidoni.com/

Photography Galleries

Andrew Smith Gallery
203 West San Francisco Street, (505) 984-1234
http://www.andrewsmithgallery.com/

Monroe Gallery of Photography
112 Don Gaspar Avenue, (505) 992-0800
http://www.monroegallery.com/

Photogenesis
100 East San Francisco Street, in La Fonda, (505) 989-9540
http://www.photogenesisgallery.com/

Scheinbaum and Russek Ltd.
Call for appointment, (505) 988-5116
http://www.photographydealers.com/

SHOPPING

Guadalupe District: Sanbusco Market Center
500 Montezuma Avenue
(505) 989-9390
If walls could talk, this building would recount some fascinating stories! Built in 1882, it was for many years part of Santa Fe's warehouse area. A 1980s renovation elevated the esthetics of the place and consequently its spirit: there's a lot going on here! You'll find excellent restaurants and wildly diverse shopping—divine temptations of all kinds.
http://www.sanbusco.com/
(Sanbusco Market Center)

The Plaza
From ancient Native artifacts to the quirkiest tourist kitsch, from designer boutiques to eclectic imports, from books to toys to postcards to—you name it! You'll find it all on or near the Plaza. In fact, perhaps the best place in town to buy Indian arts and crafts is right there, outdoors under the *portal* of the Palace of the Governors (see next page).

When you buy directly from the artists selling outside the Palace of the Governors, you are assured of authenticity and quality—and great value.

Buying Native Arts & Jewelry

The Santa Fe area presents many opportunities to purchase the best in Indian arts and crafts. Check the Pueblo events schedule on page 191; arts-and-crafts fairs are held in conjunction with many of these events, so you can visit a pueblo, enjoy some colorful Native dancing and do some shopping all in one trip. Larger fairs, such as Indian Market and the Eight Northern Indian Pueblos Council Artists and Craftsmen Show, present excellent opportunities to see and purchase some of the finest Indian art available. To learn more about what to look for and about individual artists, see these Web sites:

http://www.newmexicoindianart.org/buyingart.html
(guide to buying Indian art and jewelry)

http://www.ciaccouncil.org/
(Council for Indigenous Arts & Culture)

http://nmculturenet.org/artists/Artists_and_Artisans/New_Mexico_Pueblos_and_Tribes/
(Artists directory)

http://nmculturenet.org/artists
(CultureNetWork, an on-line directory of artists, artisans, arts organizations, galleries and others involved in the cultural life of New Mexico)

The Portal at the Palace of the Governors

As we stated, the *portal* at the Palace of the Governors is perhaps the very best place in town to buy Indian jewelry. The New Mexico Native American artists are licensed by the museum. You can meet the artists and buy direct, and you can "discuss" the price. The rules vendors must follow emphasize authenticity (a maker's mark is required on all goods), traditional materials, and handmade work produced as generations of Native artisans have created it. You can count on the quality, and the artists will be happy to tell you how each piece was created.

http://www.newmexicoindianart.org/
(Indian Art under the portal)

Shops for Native Arts & Jewelry

Adobe Gallery
221 Canyon Road, (505) 955-0550
http://www.adobegallery.com/

Andrea Fisher Fine Pottery
100 West San Francisco Street, (505) 986-1234
http://www.andreafisherpottery.com/

Cristof's
420 Old Santa Fe Trail, (877) 389-6393 or (505) 988-9881
http://www.cristofs.com/

Keshi The Zuni Connection (Fetishes)
227 Don Gaspar Avenue, (505) 989-8728
http://www.keshi.com/

Oretega's on the Plaza
101 West San Francisco Street, (505) 988-1866

Packard's
61 Old Santa Fe Trail, (505) 983-9241

The Rainbow Man
107 East Palace Avenue, (505) 982-8706
(carries American Indian antiquities as well)
http://www.collectorsguide.com/sf/g174.html
http://www.therainbowman.com/

The Rancho de Chimayó Collection
Sena Plaza Galleries, 127 East Palace Avenue, (505) 988-4526
http://www.ranchochimayo.com/

Sources for American Indian Antiquities

Canfield Gallery
414 Canyon Road, (505) 988-4199
http://www.canfieldgallery.com/

William E. Channing
805 Apodaca Hill, (505) 988-1078

Kania-Ferrin Gallery
662 Canyon Road, (505) 982-8767
http://www.collectorsguide.com/sf/g101.html

Mark Sublette Medicine Man Gallery
200 Canyon Road, (505) 820-7451
http://www.medicinemangallery.com/

Michael Smith Gallery
526 Canyon Road, (505) 995-1013
http://www.michaelsmithgallery.com/

Someone has found a new use (not a recommended one) for a lovely bowl.

Morning Star Gallery
513 Canyon Road, (505) 982-8187
http://www.morningstargallery.com/

Nedra Matteucci Galleries
1075 Paseo de Peralta, (505) 982-4631
http://www.matteucci.com/

Price-Dewey Galleries
53 Old Santa Fe Trail, (505) 982-8632
http://www.deweyltd.com/

Relics of the Old West
402 Old Santa Fe Trail, (505) 989-7663
http://www.antiques-internet.com/new-mexico/relicsoftheoldwest/

Sherwood's Spirit of America
130 Lincoln Avenue, (505) 988-1776
http://www.sherwoodsspirit.com/

Shush Yaz Trading Co.
1048 Paseo de Peralta, (505) 992-9441
http://www.shushyaz.com/santafe/santafe.htm

Museum Shops

The following site is the gateway to all four shops run by the Museum of New Mexico:

http://www.shopmuseum.com/
(Museum of New Mexico Foundation Shops)

Following are the names and addresses of all the museum shops:

Museum of Indian Arts & Culture Shop
710 Camino Lejo, (505) 982-5057
http://www.miaclab.org/visit/indexs.html
http://shopmuseum.com/mia_index.php

Palace of the Governors Shop
105 West Palace Avenue, (505) 982-3016
http://www.shopmuseum.com/pog_index.php

Museum of Fine Arts Shop
107 West Palace Avenue, (505) 476-5072
http://www.shopmuseum.com/mfa_index.php

Museum of International Folk Art Shop
706 Camino Lejo, (505) 476-1200
http://www.shopmuseum.com/ifa_index.php

Case Trading Post
Wheelwright Museum of the American Indian
704 Camino Lejo, (505) 982-4636
http://www.wheelwright.org/case_trading.html

Cowboy Boots & Other Stuff

Back at the Ranch Cowboy Boots
209 East Marcy Street, (888) 96BOOTS or (505) 989-8110
http://www.backattheranch.com/

Desert Son of Santa Fe
725 Canyon Road, (505) 982-9499

Double Take at the Ranch
319 South Guadalupe Street, (505) 820-7775

Hop A Long Boot Co.
3908 Rodeo Road, (505) 471-5570

In Santa Fe, you can find anything the working or weekend cowboy needs.

Lucchese
203 West Water Street, (800) 871-1883 or (505) 820-1883
http://www.lucchese.com/

Montecristi Custom Hat Works
322 McKenzie Street, (505) 983-9598
http://www.montecristihats.com/

Relics of the Old West
402 Old Santa Fe Trail, (505) 989-7663
http://www.antiques-internet.com/new-mexico/relicsoftheoldwest/

Rio Bravo Trading Co.
411 South Guadalupe Street, (505) 982-0230

Santa Fe Boot Co.
950½ West Cordova Road, (505) 983-8415

Tom Taylor
La Fonda, (505) 984-2232

Western Warehouse
Villa Linda Mall, (505) 471-8775
http://www.westernwarehouse.com/

Bookstores

All the museums in town have large collections of books in their respective fields for sale in their shops. If you can't find what you want, try one of the bookshops.

The Ark Spiritual Bookstore
133 Romero Street, (505) 988-3709
http://www.arkbooks.com/

Borders Books & Music
Sanbusco Market Center, 500 Montezuma Avenue, (505) 954-4707
3513 Zafarano Drive, (505) 474-9450
http://www.bordersstores.com/stores/store_pg.jsp?storeID=278

Collected Works Bookstore
208-B West San Francisco Street, (505) 988-4226
http://www.collectedworksbookstore.com/

Garcia Street Books
376 Garcia Street, (505) 986-0151
http://www.charlottejackson.com/borins.htm

On-line Bookstore
http://www.booksupermart.com/

Photo-Eye Books and Prints
376 Garcia Street, (505) 988-5152
http://www.photoeye.com/Gallery/RepresentedArtists/homepagePE.cfm

Distinctive Jewelry, Clothing & Accessories
(with emphasis on Southwestern and the eclectic)

La Bodega
667 Canyon Road, (505) 982-8043

Bodhi Bazaar
Sanbusco Market Center, 500 Montezuma Avenue, (505) 982-3880
http://www.santafestation.com/bodhibazaar

Char of Santa Fe
104 Old Santa Fe Trail, (505) 988-5969

Clarke and Clarke Asian Antiques & Tribal Arts
By appointment, (505) 984-1585
http://www.ethnoarts.com/

Origins features exceptional garments and jewelry from America's foremost designers and local artists, whom you can meet at trunk shows in the summer.

Dust in The Wind
131 East Palace Avenue, (505) 986-1155

Faircloth/Adams
Hotel Loretto, 211 Old Santa Fe Trail, (505) 982-5115

Gusterman Silversmiths
26 East Palace Avenue, (505) 982-8972
http://www.thecatalogues.com/cgi-bin/shop.pl?city=santafe&fid=
s5&vendor_id=332&category_id=106

Lewallen & Lewallen
105 East Palace Avenue, (505) 983-2657
http://www.lewallenjewelry.com/

Karen Melfi Collection
225 Canyon Road, (505) 982-3032
http://www.karenmelfi.com/

Mimosa
52 Lincoln Avenue, (505) 982-5492

Nathalie
503 Canyon Road, 988-7215

Origins
135 West San Francisco Street, (505) 988-2323

Purple Sage
110 Don Gaspar Avenue, (505) 984-0600
http://www.purplesagesantafe.com/

James Reid Ltd.
114 East Palace Avenue, (505) 988-1147
http://www.jrltd.com/

Barbara Rosen Antique Jewelry
85 West Marcy Street, (505) 992-3000

Santa Fe Dry Goods
53 Old Santa Fe Trail, (505) 983-8142

Simply Santa Fe
72 East San Francisco Street, (505) 988-3100

Spirit of the Earth
108 Don Gaspar Avenue, (505) 988-9558
http://www.spiritoftheearth.com/
http://www.thecatalogues.com/
(Follow on-screen prompts—find other shops as well)

Tresa Vorenberg
656 Canyon Road, (505) 988-7215
http://tvgoldsmiths.com/

Distinctive Shoe Shops

Goler Fine Imported Shoes
125 East Palace Avenue, (505) 982-0924
http://www.golershoes.com/

On Your Feet
530 Montezuma Avenue, (505) 983-3900

Sara's Shoes
Custom-made shoes and boots
539-A Old Santa Fe Trail, (505) 989-1777
http://www.sarasshoes.com/home.html

Street Feet
La Fonda, (505) 984-2828
221 Galisteo Street, (505) 984-3131

Walking on Water
207 West Water Street, Suite 101, (505) 820-0576

Home Furnishings, Architectural Elements & Miscellaneous

American Country Collection
Antiques, home furnishings.
620 Cerrillos Road, (505) 984-0955
53 Old Santa Fe Trail, (505) 982-1296

Antique Warehouse
Spanish colonial antiques, old doors, windows, gates.
530 South Guadalupe Street, Suite B, (505) 984-1159
http://www.resource2.com/santafe/antiquewarehouse/

Arius Tile
114 Don Gaspar Avenue, (505) 988-1196
La Fonda, (505) 988-1125
Fine hand-crafted art tile and murals.
http://www.ariustile.com/

Artesanos Imports
Tiles, ceramic sinks, iron work for the home.
222 Galisteo Street, (505) 983-1743
http://www.artesanos.com/contact.html

Bell & Dorje Tibetan Arts & Crafts
Tibetan Imports
112 West San Francisco Street, (505) 983-6863

The Clay Angel
European ceramics.
125 Lincoln Avenue, (505) 988-4800

La Compania Antique Door Co.
Fine furniture and doors.
2894 Trades West Road, (505) 471-2971

Counterpoint Tile
Contemporary tile.
320 Sandoval Street, (505) 982-1247
http://www.counterpointtile.com/

El Paso Imports
Mexican furniture (much of it crafted from old
wooden Mexican pieces), windows and gates.
419 Sandoval Street, (505) 982-5698
http://www.elpasoimportco.com/

Foreign Traders
Southwest and Spanish furniture and architectural accessories.
202 Galisteo Street, (505) 983-6441
http://www.foreigntraders.com/

Jackalope
"Everything under the sun," mainly Mexican imports and pottery.
2820 Cerrillos Road, (505) 471-8539
http://jackalopeinternational.com/santafe

La Puerta
Old doors and furniture designed from old wooden pieces.
1302 Cerrillos Road, (505) 984-8164
http://www.lapuertaoriginals.com

Santa Fe Country Furniture
Southwest furniture.
1708 Cerrillos Road, (505) 984-1478

Santa Fe Heritage
The look of antiquity in Southwestern door styles.
418 Montezuma Avenue, (505) 988-3328
http://santafeheritagedoors.com/

Seret & Sons Rugs & Furnishings
Rugs, tapestries, architectural elements, fine furnishings
224 Galisteo Street, (505)-988-9151
149 E. Alameda Street, (505) 982-3214
http://www.seretandsons.com/

The Shop, A Christmas Store
The ultimate year-round selection of exceptional ornaments.
116 East Palace Avenue, (800) 525-5764 or (505) 983-4823
http://www.theshopchristmas.com/

Simply Santa Fe
Southwestern furniture.
72 East San Francisco Street, (505) 988-3100

"One of the world's great shopping experiences." (Conde Nast) Seret & Sons fills over 50,000 square feet in two locations with one of the largest collections of rugs, doors, pillars, Tibetan furniture and one of a kind custom furnishings.

Southwest Spanish Craftsmen
Fine Spanish reproduction furniture and accessories.
328 South Guadalupe Street, (505) 982-1767

Spanish Pueblo Doors
Classic Southwest door reproductions.
1091 Siler Road, Unit B-1, (505) 473-0464
http://www.spdoors.com/Home/Default.htm

Susan's Christmas Shop
Original and handmade Christmas decorations.
115 East Palace Avenue, (505) 983-2127
http://www.susanschristmasshop.com

Taos Furniture
Customized Southwestern furniture.
219 Galisteo Street, (505) 988-1229
http://www.taosfurniture.com/

SPAS

Slip into a spa after a day of doing Santa Fe!

Avanyu Spa at La Posada de Santa Fe
330 East Palace
(505) 986-0000 or (505) 954-9630

This new spa is located on La Posada Resort grounds, just a few blocks from the Plaza. Its state-of-the-art massage center offers skin-care treatments and specialty bodywork, a fitness center, an outdoor heated pool and a whirlpool (see also pages 76 and 100).

http://laposada.rockresorts.com/info/spa.asp
(Avanyu Spa at La Posada)

Genoveva Chávez Community Center
3321 Rodeo Road
(505) 955-4001 or (505) 955-4002, call for information and directions.

If you're in the mood for a good old-fashioned workout, then the new Chávez Center is for you. It's workout heaven here with an Olympic-size pool, a full gym, a running track and a NHL regulation-size hockey and figure-skating rink. You can even rent ice skates! If you need a massage, that can be arranged with an advance call. Owned by the city, the Chávez center offers very reasonable rates for daily admission. Truly a Santa Fe jewel.

http://mazria.com/projects/gccc.html
(Chávez Community Center)
http://www.visitsantafe.com/businesspage.cfm?businessid=1957
(Chávez Center hours/fees)

Ojo Caliente Mineral Springs
North on U.S. 285
50 Los Baños Drive, Ojo Caliente, N.M.
(800) 222-9162 or (505) 583-2233
Open seven days a week, call for hours.

New Mexicans have enjoyed this spa for decades. One of the oldest health resorts in North America, it was considered a sacred spot by the Pueblo Indians who inhabited the area. These are the only natural hot springs in the world containing a specific mixture of iron, lithia, soda, arsenic and sodium. Besides a good soak, you may avail yourself of

The Big Pool at Ojo Caliente. Photo © 2003 Ojo Caliente Mineral Springs.

therapeutic massage and facial treatments, yoga instruction and guided meditations, art workshops, a restaurant, gift shop, hiking trails, and hotel and cottage lodging.

http://ojocalientespa.com/
(Ojo Caliente)

SháNah Spa at Bishop's Lodge

Bishop's Lodge Road (10 minutes from downtown, call for directions)
(505) 983-6377 or (800) 732-2240

The SháNah Spa at The Bishop's Lodge is located in the lush foothills just north of Santa Fe, which is steeped deep within the Native American traditions and home of some of the oldest Spanish settlements in America. With these strong traditions, SháNah makes use of natural healing remedies, herbs, sweat baths and teas. They aim to customize the treatment to each individual, invoking the body's natural healing response. From Native Stone Massage to the Tesuque Clay Wrap, Abiyanga to Desert Fusion, the treatments go beyond your highest expectations (see also page 101).

http://www.bishopslodge.com/
(Bishop's Lodge)
http://www.shanahspa.com/shanah/
(SháNah Spa at Bishop's Lodge)

Sunrise Springs Inn & Retreat
242 Los Pinos Road
La Cienega, N.M.
(505) 471-3600, call for information and rates.

This laid-back spot is only 12 miles from Santa Fe, but you'd swear you'd traveled more like 12,000 miles! The feeling is Far Eastern, and the emphasis is on massage, yoga and ancient wellness treatments. The accommodations are lovely, the views are beautiful and the dining is very, very fine (see also page 102).

http://www.ibbp.com/obb/newmexico/sunrisesprings.html
(Sunrise Springs)
http://www.sunrisesprings.com/livingcenter/spa.htm
(Sunrise Springs spa)

Tamaya Mist Spa
Hyatt Regency Tamaya Resort & Spa
1300 Tuyuna Trail
Santa Ana Pueblo, N.M.
(800) 633-7313 or (505) 867-1234

The Pueblo-style, luxurious 16,000-square-foot spa features specialty treatments, massage, skin treatments and more. It also offers a well-equipped fitness center and a beautiful yoga/aerobic wellness theater. Separate men's and women's meditation, sauna/steam and changing areas add to the relaxed enjoyment of this world-class spa. In addition to our luxury spa treatments it offers many specialty classes and pro-grams, including world-class yoga instruction, specialized fitness classes, one-on-one personal training, tai chi and meditation events.

http://tamaya.hyatt.com/property/hotelinfo/inhouse/index.jhtml
(Tamaya Mist Spa)

Ten Thousand Waves
3451 Hyde Park Road
(505) 982-9304, call for directions and hours.
We first found this particularly wonderful spa in the mid-1980s. I well remember our private room—open to the beauty of the Sangre de Cristo Mountains—and the satisfying hot tub and superb Swedish massage that followed.

Ten Thousand Waves has since evolved into a state-of-the-art Japanese health spa with all the amenities—therapeutic massages as well as specialized types including Masters, Thai, Japanese Hot Stone and Four Hands (two therapists working in union). Healthy snacks and drinks can be purchased along with creams and lotions, candles and cotton kimonos. Oh my!

This is primarily a day spa, but with luck, you may be able to reserve one of their luxurious guest suites at the Houses of the Moon—the closest accommodations to the Santa Fe Ski Area.

http://www.tenthousandwaves.com/
(Ten Thousand Waves)

Vista Clara Ranch Resort and Spa
Route 41, Galisteo, N.M.
(888) 663-9772 or (505) 466-4772
Call for information and rates.

About one-half hour out of Santa Fe, just outside the tiny artsy village of Galisteo you'll find the Vista Clara Ranch. Vista Clara offers upscale lodging and gourmet cuisine complementing its spa treatments and therapies, an ozone pool, jacuzzi, Swiss showers, art classes and a sweat lodge . . . the works. And don't forget hiking, horseback riding and a gym—if you've got the strength. You can even arrange for a limo to pick you up and take you home. Wow!

http://www.vistaclara.com/
(Vista Clara Ranch Resort and Spa)

SIDE TRIPS
TO THE COUNTRY

One of the best parts of visiting Santa Fe is the variety of "must do" day trips out into the surrounding countryside. You'll come away with an enhanced sense of local history and some treasured memories of the beauty of the land. We're aware that your visit here may be a short one, and thus have only listed those trips that are reasonably close to Santa Fe. Onward!

http://www.newmexico.org/ScenicAttractions/
(New Mexico scenic attractions)
http://www.newmexico.org/outdoors/
(New Mexico sports and outdoors)

ABUQUIÚ

Most of us have become aware of the beauty of the hills and canyons of Abiquiú through the landscape paintings of Georgia O'Keeffe. The Abiquiú area is most assuredly a fine day's trip.

http://www.okeeffemuseum.org/background/
(Georgia O'Keeffe Museum)

O'Keeffe was artistically inspired by Abiquiú and in 1949 moved there permanently. Long before she arrived, legends of witches or *brujos* were widely circulated. In Lesley Poling-Kempes' wonderful history book, *Valley of Shining Stone: The Story of Abiquiú*, she notes:

> *In a region already rich in superstition—the local lore of the Piedra Lumbre included tales of a flying cow who heralded not just insanity but also imminent death, and an oft repeated legend of a giant, child-eating snake that emerged from the earth near the red cliffs at sundown—the Archuleta brothers and their homestead beneath the cliffs of Shining Stone would earn legendary*

Left: Bandelier National Monument combines historic Indian ruins with magnificent scenery and hiking trails.

If you wish to spend more than a day in Georgia O'Keeffe country, you can stay at the Abiquiú Inn. Photo ©Karen T. Bartlett.

From Santa Fe, take U.S. 285 north to Española. At Española, pick up U.S. 84 North and follow it toward Abiquiú. After reaching Abiquiú, you will enter a 15-mile stretch that encompasses Ghost Ranch and the world of Georgia O'Keeffe.

status... they chose this hidden canyon with its singular southern entrance and sheer rock walls because of its natural characteristic as a holding and hiding pen for cattle. According to local legend the Archuleta brothers herded stolen cattle through the mountains by day and the valleys by night to their secluded, natural rock canal in Yeso Canyon... out of towners who stopped for the night for what they thought was friendly and welcomed lodging... never emerged in the morning and their horses and personal effects were suddenly counted among the Archuletas' tack and livestock. The corpses of the victims were believed to be at the bottom of the homestead well. The Rito del Yeso homestead was soon given a new name: Rancho de los Brujos, or Witch Ranch, or Ghost Ranch. (Poling-Kempes, p. 129)

That piece of land is still Ghost Ranch. It is now owned by the Presbyterian Church, which operates it as a conference center. Georgia O'Keeffe had a home at Ghost Ranch named Rancho de los Burros. Ghost Ranch mainly hosts conferences, but individual rooms may be available. For inquires call (505) 685-4333 or access the Ghost Ranch Web site.

http://www.ghostranch.org/
(Ghost Ranch Conference Center)

Georgia O'Keeffe had another, more famous home in Abiquiú itself. She lived there from 1949 to 1984. It is now run by the O'Keeffe Foundation, which conducts limited tours of the 7,000-square-foot adobe. The simplicity of the house and its rooms reflect the aesthetic soul of the artist. Tours are by reservation only and must be scheduled well in advance. They are held on Tuesdays, Thursdays and Fridays from April through November, generally for up to 12 people. A fee donation of $22 is requested and is tax-deductible. For further information contact the Georgia O'Keeffe Foundation, P.O. Box 40, Abiquiú, NM 87510, (505) 685-4539.

http://www.cr.nps.gov/nr/feature/wom/1999/o'keeffe.htm
(Georgia O'Keeffe Home and Studio)

After 1984 O'Keeffe moved to Santa Fe to be closer to medical facilities. Her estate, called "Sol y Sombre" (Sun and Shade), was occupied until her death in 1986 at age 98.

http://www.natsys-inc.com/topics/examples/vc/sombre/sombre.html
(Sol y Sombre Conference Center)

Also of interest in Abiquiú is the Monastery of Christ in the Desert, run by the Subiaco Monastic Community headquartered in Rome, Italy. It is a simple retreat with a lovely church and a refectory adorned with magnificent religious frescoes. The original church architect is George Nakashima, a world-renowned artist.

http://www.christdesert.org/
(Monastery of Christ in the Desert)

In Abiquiú, the Abiquiú Inn has been welcome respite from touring since 1985, offering lodging, an R.V. park and a pleasant restaurant. Call (800)-477-5621.

http://www.abiquiuinn.com/
(Abiquiú Inn)

BANDELIER NATIONAL MONUMENT

Near Los Alamos, N.M.

(505) 672-3861

The monument is 46 miles (74.1 km) west of Santa Fe. Take U.S. 285 north from Santa Fe north to Pojoaque, then drive west on N.M. 502 to N.M. State Road 4 (12 miles southwest of Los Alamos). The volcano that erupted on this land so long ago formed one of the largest "calderas," or depressions, in the world; the volcanic rim forms the Jemez Mountains. On these canyon-slashed slopes at the bottom of the Pajarito Plateau you will see the ruins of cliff houses and pueblo-style dwellings of 13th-century Pueblo Indians. Bandelier is a 32,000-acre monument to the Anasazis who once lived there as well as to Adolph Bandelier, a Swiss-American ethnologist who studied Southwest pueblo ruins in the late 19th century. Within Bandelier, 70 miles of trails provide access to ancient pueblos, cliff dwellings and ceremonial caves and offer as well opportunities for backpacking, bird watching, camping and picnicking. Bandelier is not to be missed!

http://www.nps.gov/band/

(Bandelier National Monument)

http://www.desertusa.com/ban/

(Bandelier National Monument)

http://www.desertusa.com/ban/du_bandesc.html

(Bandelier cultural history)

http://www.nmculture.org/cgi-bin/instview.cgi?_recordnum=BAND

(Bandelier addresses and contacts)

http://emuseum.mnsu.edu/information/biography/abcde/bandelier_adolph.html

(Adolph Bandelier)

TENT ROCKS NATIONAL MONUMENT

(800) 252-0191

Spectacular and unusual land formations can be found at Tent Rocks.

To get there, take I-25 south to the Cochiti exit (264). At the end of the exit ramp go right on N.M. 16 for 8 miles. At the 'T' intersection turn right onto N.M. 22.

Go 1.7 miles and then turn right on Tribal Rd. 92/ Forest Service Rd. 266. Pass through a gate and continue for 5 miles to the parking area on the right. You'll see a sign saying 'Welcome to Tent Rocks.' The fee is $5 per vehicle.

Do you remember making those wonderful sandcastles at the beach? No matter how you tried to preserve them, the tide came in and wiped them out. Fret no more. Tent Rocks is a place where castles don't disappear. It's a place where 6.8 million years ago, volcanic rock debris formations were sculpted into tent-like cones. Covering almost 12,000 acres, Tent Rocks is a dry place and good for hiking—to be avoided in the summer months, however, when it heats up. Try the 1.1-mile Cave Loop Hike or Canyon Trail, a 1.3-mile jaunt with a modest elevation gain. Kids will love it and so will you.

http://www.recreation.gov/detail.cfm?ID=(3118

(Tent Rocks)

http://www.electrickiva.com/gregmalone/tentrocks/tentrocks_01.htm

(photo of Tent Rocks)

Winter on the Turquoise Trail.

THE TURQUOISE TRAIL

As a counterbalance to "'Santa Fe adobe," why not experience a short journey out of the city to two towns that reveal another side of New Mexico? Cerrillos and Madrid (accent the *Ma* to pronounce it as New Mexicans do) will transport you into yet another realm of New Mexican history and architecture.

http://www.turquoisetrail.org/
(Turquoise Trail)
http://www.byways.org/image_library/summary_list.html?CX_COLL=118
(about Turquoise Trail)
http://www.newmexico.org/ScenicAttractions/byway_turq.html
(about Turquoise Trail)
http://www.byways.org/travel/byway.html?CX_BYWAY=2094
(about Turquoise Trail)

Cerrillos

Take I-25 south to the Madrid exit (278A), moving onto Route 14 going south. Drive for about 20 minutes (15 miles).

Visit Cerrillos to see a town that still looks like the turn of the century.

Cerrillos is an old mining town where people settled and dug for gold, silver, zinc and the best quality turquoise in the surrounding hills. Its quiet demeanor today hardly reveals its rowdy 1880s roots when it was filled with hotels and bars. A street or two are still reminiscent of that frontier town, but now the main attractions are a turquoise museum, a petting zoo, a trading post and a church, the Iglesia San Jose, built in 1922. A now faded sign painted on the side of a brick building—"Clear Light Opera House"—conjures up the Cerrillos of days gone by.

http://www.ghosttowns.com/states/nm/cerillos.html
(Cerrillos)
http://htg-is.vianet.net/~artpike/cerril15.htm
(historic photo of turquoise mine at Cerrillos)
http://www.cerrilloshills.org
(Cerrillos Hills Historic Park)

Allan Houser Compound
(505) 471-1528, call for directions and hours.

After leaving Cerrillos, continue south on Route 14, turning left onto Route 42 towards Galisteo, and in 1.5 miles you will come upon the Allan Houser Compound.

To arrange a visit, please call two days in advance. Tours are Monday through Saturday and cost $15 per person. Allow two hours at this remarkable place.

Allan Houser (Allan C. Haozous) was a renowned Chiricahua Apache sculptor (1914–1994). His works are to be found in numerous museums including the National Museum of American Art in Washington, D.C., The Denver Art Museum and the Heard Museum in Phoenix, Arizona. His statue, *Sacred Rain Arrow*, done in 1988, was on display during the 2002 Winter Olympics in Salt Lake City, Utah. The compound and gardens that house much of Houser's work are absolutely worth the trip.

http://www.allanhouser.com/intro.html
(Allan Houser)

Madrid

This row of frame houses was once occupied by miners.

This small, colorful place was originally a coal-mining town that began to boom in the 1860s. The mines uniquely produced both hard and soft coal and Madrid thrived into the World War II years when coal was much needed. By 1959, other fuels had replaced the "indispensable" coal, and the town was left with 12 people. The Old Coal Mine Museum is a worthwhile visit.

http://www.turquoisetrail.org/oldcoalmine/
(Old Coal Mine Museum)
http://htg-is.vianet.net/~artpike/turq9.htm
(photos of old coal mine in Madrid)

In the 1970s, Madrid was reinvented by artists and crafts people looking for an inexpensive lifestyle. Today, it boasts an artist colony of about 350 people. Reconverted miners' bungalows and once-vacant stores house the many galleries that sell art, weavings, ceramics and other crafts. Inside one gallery and bookstore, an original 1930s soda fountain is still in use. During the holidays, Madrid presents annual Christmas light displays on houses and stores, a lovely sight if you happen to be in Santa Fe for the holidays.

http://www.mad-rid.com/
(Madrid, New Mexico – Artist Haven)
http://www.turquoisetrail.org/madrid.htm
(Madrid)
http://www.ghosttowns.com/states/nm/madrid.html
(Madrid photos)

PECOS

Walking around the ruins at Pecos National Historical Park, you can see far-away vistas in every direction, as if you are on the top of the world.

Go out I-25 north to the Glorieta/Pecos exit, then cross the highway and turn left towards Pecos. When you get to town, you can go left and up into the mountains or right and head out to the Pecos National Monument. Or you may wish to spend some time in this old Northern New Mexico village itself!

If you are interested in seeing some magnificent scenery or in excellent fishing and hiking, take the short drive out to Pecos.

http://pecosnewmexico.com/
(Village of Pecos Web site)

Pecos National Historical Park

One of the most spectacular ruins to be seen anywhere in the nation, Pecos National Historical Park preserves 12,000 years of history, including the ancient Pueblo of Pecos. Be sure to bring your camera!

http://www.nps.gov/peco/
(Pecos National Historical Park)

Glorieta National Battlefield

On the way to Pecos, you will pass through the Glorieta National Battlefield, where a major battle of the Civil War (the Battle of Glorieta Pass, known as the "Gettysburg of the West") was fought. The Union

The highway leading to the Pecos Wilderness takes you through some of the most magnificent scenery you will see anywhere. Photo ©CassieO'Shea.

won and, thereby, stopped Confederate incursions into the Southwest and prevented the Confederates from journeying on to Colorado and its precious gold, which would have helped finance their war.

http://www2.cr.nps.gov/abpp/battles/nm002.htm
(Battle of Glorieta Pass)

http://www.npca.org/across_the_nation/npca_in_the_field/southwest/glorieta.asp
(Battle of Glorieta Pass, in depth)

http://americancivilwar.com/statepic/nm/nm002.html
(Battle of Glorieta Pass)

http://www.cr.nps.gov/nr/twhp/wwwlps/lessons/91glorieta/91glorieta.htm
(Battle of Glorieta Pass in depth)

WINERIES

New Mexico's sun-soaked soil, cool high-desert nights and ideal soil feed Cabernet Sauvignon, Chardonnay, Johannisburg Riesling, Merlot, Pinot Noir, Sauvignon Blanc, Zinfandel and other classic grapes and fruits to produce award-winning wines. Why not add dropping by a local winery to your excursion in the country? You can use this Web site to learn all about the wineries and which one may be right on your way!

http://nmwine.net/
(New Mexico Wine Growers Association)

THE GREAT OUT OF DOORS

The Rió Grande on the way to Taos.

The Santa Fe area is a wonderland for the outdoors enthusiast. Whatever your pleasure, from fishing to snowboarding, you can find it here.

http://www.santafe.com/biz/outdoors.html

(Web sites to learn more about biking, rafting, skiing, golf and hiking)

http://www.santafeinformation.com/outdoors.html

(information about hiking, biking, hunting, fishing and winter sports)

Golf

This book was written for the short-time visitor, so I was apprehensive about putting in information on golfing in Santa Fe. But my golfing friends informed me that a golfing aficionado will always try to get in 18 holes in any city that he or she might visit, regardless of what else that city has to offer. So with that, here are some selections for nearby golf:

http://www.golfnewmexico.com/

(Golf New Mexico Magazine)

http://www.nmgolf.net/

(where to go in New Mexico)

http://www.newmexico.org/outdoors/golf_reg.html

(find all the courses in New Mexico)

Black Mesa Golf Club
115 State Road 399
La Mesilla, N.M.
(505) 747-8946

Owned by Santa Clara Pueblo, Northern New Mexico's newest 18-hole championship course is located about 30 miles from Santa Fe. Take U.S. 84/285 north, go west on N.M. 399 at the Dream Catcher Cinema, then turn south after less than a mile. You will find a gravel driveway and a gate that says Black Mesa. For refreshments, you can enjoy burritos and burgers at the Black Mesa Grill.

http://www.blackmesagolfclub.com/
(Black Mesa Golf Club)

Marty Sanchez Links de Santa Fe
205 Caja del Rio
(505) 955-4400

Right at the edge of town lies a beautiful public 28-hole championship course and a 9-hole par 3 course, all framed by the Sangre de Cristo, Jemez, Sandia and Ortiz mountains.

http://www.golfnewmexico.com/pages/courses/martysanchez.html
(Marty Sanchez Links)
http://www.travelgolf.com/sanchez1.htm
(Marty Sanchez Links)
http://www.us-discount-golf.com/mar-nac/Marty_Sanchez_Links.html
(Marty Sanchez Links discounts)

Santa Fe Country Club
On Airport Road, 2 miles west of Cerrillos Road
(505) 471-0601

The Santa Fe Country Club has a challenging 18-hole course that is now available for public play. Call for tee times and information.

http://www.visitsantafe.com/businesspage.cfm?businessid=1781
Santa Fe Country Club golf information

Towa Golf Resort
U.S. 84/285, Pojoaque Pueblo
(877) 465-3489 or (505) 455-9000

Towa Golf Resort offers challenging golf, amazing Southwestern vistas and first-rate service. Eighteen of the 36 holes, designed by Hale Irwin and William Phillips, are now open, as well as a first-class clubhouse and golf shop that features a full-service restaurant and bar complete with meeting facilities. Located at Pojoaque Pueblo, 12 scenic miles north of Santa Fe on U.S. 84/285, Towa already has become one of the top public golf courses in the Southwest. If not everyone in your party wishes to play golf, several Pueblo casinos in the area can keep them occupied (see page 188)!

http://www.towagolf.com/

(Towa Golf Resort)

Spectacular vistas like this are no more than 10–15 minutes from downtown.

Hiking

Remembering that this book was designed for the person on a short visit, you might feel hard-pressed to get away to the dirt, gravel and pine needles of the hiking trails of Santa Fe. But for those of you so inclined there are several hikes I would suggest. Once you get up into the Sangre de Cristos with their piñons, junipers and ponderosa pines, you will feel for certain that you're in the Rocky Mountains of Colorado.

Remember to always take water and appropriate clothing (including a hat) as the weather can change abruptly at any season of the year. Also be aware of the altitude; most of the mountain trails are considerably higher than Santa Fe's 7,000-foot elevation. As you climb, you may feel short of breath. It does take a day or two to acclimate to the altitude. Here are four of my favorite close-to-town hikes that will get you out into nature and onto the trails.

http://www.santafe.com/biz/outdoors/hiking.html

(descriptions of local hiking trails)

Hikers of all experience levels will enjoy the Atalaya Trail.

Atalaya Mountain

This seven-mile round trip hike begins at the parking lot right next to St. John's College. Walk at your own pace, and as you climb higher, keep turning around to enjoy the views of the Rio Grande Valley and the city of Santa Fe below you and the Jemez Mountains to the west. The trail winds through piñon and juniper, ponderosa, Douglas and white fir trees. It's about 3½ miles from the parking lot to the top of Atalaya ("watchtower"), and at the top you're at 9,121 feet, with a spectacular view spread out before you. Even if you don't make it all the way to the top, you will be rewarded with magnificent views wherever you choose to stop.

From the northeast corner of the Plaza, drive east (toward the mountains) on Palace Avenue for one mile, cross Paseo de Peralta and continue to the intersection of Palace and Alameda. Turn left on Alameda Street. A few hundred yards past Smith Park, Alameda veers right (south) and becomes Camino Cabra. Continue south on Camino Cabra past Cristo Rey Catholic Church. About 0.7 mile past Cristo Rey Catholic Church, you'll pass Los Miradores condo development on your left. Turn left onto Camino Cruz Blanca at the St. John's College sign. Turn right into St. John's College then left into the visitors parking lot. Trailhead #174 is at the far end of the lot.

All of the area hiking trails provide magnificent views.

Aspen Vista

From the Plaza, go north on Washington Avenue, cross Paseo de Peralta and up ahead, turn right at Artist Road. The sign here will point you to Hyde State Park and the Ski Basin. Follow this road (SH 475) 12.6 miles (uphill) from there and turn right into the parking lot with the Aspen Vista sign.

This is a wide-open trail that Santa Feans use for hiking, snow shoeing, cross-country skiing and mountain biking. It can be easy or strenuous, depending... the entire trail is a 12-mile round trip, but many people use it for a simple, strolling hike. It is especially beautiful in the autumn—October is best—when the aspens make their magic by turning a brilliant yellow (hence the name of the trail). Allow six hours if you're going to do the entire hike. The highest point of the trail is 12,040 feet, and the elevation gain is 2,040 feet.

Chamisa Trail

From town, go north on Washington Avenue and turn right on Artist Road. The sign here will point you to Hyde State Park and the Ski Basin. Follow this road (SH 475) for approximately 5.6 miles to a wide spot on the left side of the road and park there. You will find a U.S. Forest sign marked Trail 183–Big Tesuque 2¼ miles. Begin here

This is a 4¾-mile round trip, a rather easy hike that will take you through beautiful, sweet-smelling piñon-juniper and mixed conifer vegetation belts, with a rise in elevation of 1,240 feet. Descending, you arrive at Big Tesuque Creek on the ski basin road. Be sure to bring a hat!

The Randall Davey Audubon Center
1800 Upper Canyon Road
(505) 983-4609

The Center is at the end of Upper Canyon Road. Head up Canyon Road and on through the residential area until you see Cristo Rey Catholic Church on your right. Turn right at the church, then turn immediately to the left and continue driving to the end of the road.

Randall Davey, one of Santa Fe's favorite painters of the early and mid-1900s, bought this historic old house and the 135-acre grounds in 1920. The National Audubon Society purchased the property from the Randall Davey Foundation in 1983 and now maintains the grounds as an environmental education center and wildlife refuge. The property was once a Spanish land grant; later it became the U.S. Army's sawmill. Located at the mouth of the Santa Fe Canyon, the sanctuary includes miles of gorgeous hiking trails and boasts as well a small pond and wetland area, a picnic area, gardens, orchards and a lawn area. One may tour the home (reservations are necessary), peruse the small, delightful gift shop and then take to the trails to learn about the flora and fauna of Northern New Mexico.

http://www.abqjournal.com/go/trails/trail11-19-98.htm
(Randall Davey Audubon Center)

http://www.audubon.org/chapter/nm/nm/rdac/body.html
(Randall Davey Audubon Center)

Horseback Riding

Thoughts of the Southwest usually conjure up thoughts of cowboys, horses and wide-open spaces. Santa Fe and its environs can provide the horses should you want to get up and ride in the saddle. You can contact these places for prices and reservations:

Alta Vista Stables
54½ East San Francisco Street
(505) 983-6565

Bishop's Lodge Ranch Resort
Bishop's Lodge Road
(505) 983-6377
Rides from April to October
http://www.bishopslodge.com/horseback.cfm
(horseback riding at Bishop's Lodge)

Trail riding is a great way to see the country.
Photo ©Broken Saddle Riding Company

The next two can be combined with a trip down the Turquoise Trail:

Makarios Ranch
Galisteo Basin
(505) 473-1038
http://members.aol.com/annieokl/rides.index.html
(Makarios Ranch)

Broken Saddle Riding Company
Off N.M. 14, Cerrillos
(505) 424-7774
http://www.brokensaddle.com
(Broken Saddle Riding Company)

River Rafting

Santa Fe is not far from the Rió Grande and the Rió Chama. With the first rush of snowmelt in early May, the rafting and kayaking season begins and runs through the summer. Early spring brings fast water and big waves. By midsummer, the rivers calm down and the runs are easier and more playful. Rafting is a good way to take in the natural beauty of New Mexico. On the next page are some of the rafting companies to contact, should you have the inclination and the time.

Rafting trips range from family floats to thrilling white-water adventures.

Kokopelli Rafting
541 West Cordova Road
(800) 879-9035 or (505) 983-3734
http://www.kokopelliraft.com/
(Kokopelli Rafting)

New Wave Rafting Company
Route 5, Box 302A
(800) 984-1444 or (505) 984-1444
http://www.newwaverafting.com/
(New Wave Rafting Company)

Rio Grande River Tours
U.S. 84/285 to S.R. 68, Pilar
(800) 525-4966 or (505) 758-0762
http://www.rivertours.com/
(Rio Grande River Tours)

Santa Fe Rafting Company & Outfitters
P.O. Box 23535
(800) 467-7238 or (505) 988-4914
http://www.santaferafting.com/
(Santa Fe Rafting Company)

Rio Grande River Adventures
(800) 983-7756
http://www.knownworldguides.com/rio.html
(Rio Grande River Adventures)

Skiing the "Burn" at the Santa Fe Ski Area. Photo ©Don Strel.

Winter Sports

Skiing and Snowboarding

Santa Fe Ski Area

(505) 983-9155 and (505) 982-4429

If you're visiting in the winter and love to ski, it's smart to be ready and bring your own skis. Or, if you prefer, you can rent equipment at one of many shops in town or at the ski valley itself. Santa Fe has a jewel of a ski basin just 16 miles from the Plaza. Trails are beautifully groomed, and the snow averages 200 inches annually. Trails cater to every type of skier, and the views are magnificent.

http://www.skisantafe.com/
(Ski Santa Fe)

Snowshoeing and Cross-Country Skiing

Two hiking trails mentioned previously, Chamisa Trail and Aspen Vista Trail, make ideal snowshoeing trails in the winter (see page 143). Bring your own shoes or rent them at various sport shops listed in the Yellow Pages. Snowshoeing offers blessed solitude, stellar views a great aerobic workout, and, of course, the trails are free! They are also great for cross-country skiing; just remember that there isn't much flat terrain in the Santa Fe area—it's important to master the art of snowplowing for stopping on a downhill trail.

TAOS

Tourists have always been lured from Santa Fe to spend at least a day in Taos. Although a much smaller town (population about 7,000), it is similar to Santa Fe in its rich Spanish history, thriving art colony, famous Indian pueblo and, of course, its world-class ski complex.

From Santa Fe, there are two basic ways to get to Taos. The first, the Low Road along the rushing Rió Grande, and the second, the High Road, which takes you into the higher country, where you can see the small villages, visit the famous Santuario de Chimayó, and perhaps buy a beautiful weaving. The round trip can be a loop, so you can do both in a day. We recommend you start your journey by following the High Road, as it is longer and has more attractions along the way.

"You take the high road, and I'll take the low road..." are the words we all know from an old Scottish song—but those words can easily apply to your trip to Taos. The roads you'll travel are some of the most scenic in the United States.

http://www.taoschamber.com/index.php3
(Taos County Chamber of Commerce)
http://www.taosguide.com/
(Guide to Taos)
http://taosWebb.com/
(Taos Visitors' Guide)
http://taosvacationguide.com/
(Taos Vacation Guide)
http://www.skitaos.org/
(Taos Ski Valley)

Left: Spectacular mountain scenery dominates the skyline near Taos.

THE HIGH ROAD TO TAOS

The old wooden doorway welcomes you to the Santuario de Chimayó.

We start by taking U.S. 84/285 north out of Santa Fe. Several miles before Española, you will come to N.M. 503. Turn right on 503, which heads north and east, and you will begin your High Road adventure! The first stop of this journey is Chimayó. Make a left turn onto N.M. 76 and follow the signs to Chimayó.

http://www.evanderputten.org/special/newmexico/highroad.htm
(High Road to Taos)
http://www.nationalgeographic.com/destinations/Taos/High_Road_to_Taos_Scenic_Drive.html
(High Road to Taos)

Chimayó
The Santuario de Chimayó
One of the main reasons for visiting Chimayó is to see its church, the Santuario de Chimayó. A Chimayó family built this chapel around 170 years ago. It resembles Spanish mission churches, except the church is smaller, the bell towers are partly wood and a low building masks the front. The main roof is pitched and of corrugated metal, typical of later Northern New Mexican. The setting is very rural, with cows grazing nearby, the *acequia* [ditch] in front, the stream behind, the fruit trees in the valley and the mountains as a backdrop.

The late Edward C. Clark, a longtime resident of Santa Fe, described the Santuario de Chimayó and the town as follows:

This chapel is no museum, no ordinary church. It is the Lourdes of the Southwest. On Good Friday, thousands of Hispanics and Indians come here, some traveling hundreds of miles. Many of them walk from Santa Fe, from Albuquerque, from even more distant spots. Nearby highways become crowded with pilgrims. Some bear heavy crosses, a few walk on their knees, most get blisters. The beaten grass, the picnic tables, the outdoor altar behind the chapel, the several nearby stores only partly reflect the crowds —it's exhilarating, not peaceful, then.

Pilgrims come here to fulfill vows and to pray for cures. One focal point is a posito, or little well in the floor inside. Dirt scooped from that hole has long been credited with miraculous cures, perhaps even before there was a chapel. The posito may, in fact, perpetuate an earlier Tewa Indian belief that the site had curative powers. There is plenty of blessed dirt nearby, but on Good Friday, and in July on the feast day of Santiago (St. James), church aides are hard-pressed to keep the posito full.

http://www.roadsideamerica.com/attract/NMCHIshrine.html
(The Lourdes of America)
http://www.archdiocesesantafe.org/AboutASF/Chimayó.html
(El Santuario de Chimayó, the Lourdes of America)

Shops and Gallery

After visiting the chapel, drive one mile north on N.M. 510. You will see a sign on the left describing Chimayó. Make a sharp left, passing in front of Ortega's Weaving Shop. Consider stopping there if you have time—their woolen weavings are a traditional Chimayó specialty. Go 1/10 of a mile and bear right at Casa Feliz. The Casa Feliz Gallery & Chimayó Southwestern Gift Shop has been the home of the Luis Martinez family since 1908. If you have time, you may want to visit these shops.

http://www.visitsantafe.com/businesscard.cfm?businessid=1074
(Ortega's Weaving Shop)
http://www.casafelizgallery.com/
(Casa Feliz Gallery)
http://www.chimayomuseum.org/
(The Chimayó Museum)

A typical home near Chimayó, with its adobe walls, *ristras* and dog.

Plaza and Presidio

Just ahead at the "Y," turn left and pass between the houses into Chimayó Plaza. Some land is farmed, so don't go beyond the houses on the far side of the planted areas. Please be respectful—the homes and grounds are private.

These plaza buildings, with their thick outside walls, were originally constructed with few windows. Torreons, or defense towers, guarded the corners. One still stands. In case of Indian attack, residents could bring in the livestock, close the gates, man the roofs and sit tight. Water from Santa Fe's presidio came in by the acequia, which is still flowing. Residents could grow crops and store grains there. The plaza/fort could hold out until help came or until the Indians gave up.

After the Indian raids ended, the presidio served no purpose. People spread out, and a Presbyterian school and church moved in and made converts. Later, public schools replaced most Presbyterian schools, but in Chimayó the school continues to thrive. Over time, families divided the central plaza into ever-smaller plots. The form of the presidio remains, however, one of the last in the Southwest.

In 1986 Robert Redford thought Chimayó the ideal spot to film his Milagro Beanfield War, *an amusing tale of tradition vs. development in Northern New Mexico. Some residents objected, so Redford switched the filming to Truchas (see next page). Truchas made money. Chimayó kept its plaza pure. A post-Redford bumper sticker reads, "Plaza del Cerro, I love you the way you are."*

http://chimayó.org/
(Chimayó main Web site)
http://chimayó.org/history.html
(a brief history of Chimayó)
http://chimayó.org/today.html
(Chimayó today)
http://www.edd.state.nm.us/FILM/
(New Mexico Film Office)
http://chimayó.org/learn_more.html
(more about Chimayó today)

Restaurante Rancho de Chimayó
Ct. Rd. 98, Chimayó
(505) 351-4444, (505) 984-2100 or (505) 351-1211
After returning to the highway, turn right on N.M. 520 toward the Santuario, and at 0.6 mile, turn left into Restaurante Rancho de Chimayó. The Jaramillo family made this building their home 100 years ago. Later, their descendents converted it to a restaurant. You'll find the food and atmosphere a country-style masterpiece. Enjoy the terraces out back in summer, soak up patio sunshine in spring and fall and move up to the unique double fireplace on winter evenings. Eat your fill of native dishes. Do your own looking around. It's all pleasant. It's all Chimayó. (Clark, n.p.)

http://www.ranchochimayo.com/Ranchodechimayorestaurant.htm
(Rancho de Chimayó Restaurante)

Cordova

Now continue north on N.M. 76 through rolling hills and verdant forest. You will next approach Cordova, a small village that has gained a reputation for fine woodcarving over the years. A man named José Dolores Lopez created the unpainted "Cordova style" of carving in the 1920s. In the village, you will find many houses whose residents offer their carvings for sale. Also, the St. Anthony of Padua Chapel, filled with *retablos* (depictions of various saints painted on boards) is worth a peek.

This old church at Las Trampas looks much the same today
as it did centuries ago.

Truchas

The next village on the High Road is Truchas (trout, in Spanish). This
very old, very Hispanic mountain town (founded in 1754) gained some
notoriety as the location for the filming of Robert Redford's *The
Milagro Beanfield War*, based on the novel by John Nichols, a New
Mexican resident. The picture has become a movie classic.

Truchas has a sublimely creative soul—many artists are in residence and the town has several outstanding art galleries. The views of
the Sangre de Cristo Mountains from Truchas are breathtaking.

http://www.edd.state.nm.us/FILM/
(New Mexico Film Office)
**http://www.colorado.edu/EthnicStudies/ethnicstudiesjournal/
Current%20Issue/milagro_beanfield_war.htm**
(Locating the Milagro Beanfield War in Early Twentieth Century New Mexico)

Las Trampas

It's five miles to Las Trampas, a small town sprinkled with Northern
New Mexican farmhouses and stacked woodpiles. There you'll find a
wonderful mid-1700s Spanish colonial chapel, San Jose de Gracias,
which holds quite a collection of religious folk art. In 1990 William de
Buys and Alex Harris wrote *River of Traps*, or *Rió de las Trampas*, based

on the real-life story of a village resident and his influence on the lives
of the authors. If Las Tampas opens your heart, then look for the book
back in Santa Fe.

On into Taos

N.M. 76 continues up toward the fertile valley of Peñasco. Atop this
valley lies the Picuris Indian reservation (see page 172). At this juncture
follow N.M. 518 north towards Taos. Soon you'll be soaking in the mag-
nificence of the Carson National Forest. Look for the Cantonment
Burguin, set up after the Taos Revolt (1847) against American forces.
The village of Talpa comes right before 518 intersects with N.M. 68.
Make a right and continue up towards the town of Taos.

http://www.fs.fed.us/r3/carson/
(USDA Forest Service—Carson National Forest)
http://sangres.com/forest/carson.htm
(Carson National Forest)
http://www.8northern.org/picuris.php
(Picuris Pueblo)

THE LOW ROAD TO TAOS

The "low road" is the highway; take U.S. 84/285 north out of Santa Fe.
You'll pass The Santa Fe Opera and the Tesuque Pueblo Flea Market on
your left (see pages 46 and 54), and you'll be treated to the beauty of the
Sangre de Cristo Mountains in a glorious panorama laid out before you.

http://sangres.com/sitemap.htm
(Sangre de Cristo Mountains)

Española and Velarde

Continue through Española, a city even older than Santa Fe, moving
onto N.M. 68 (U.S. 84/285 diverges to the left and leads to Abiquiú, yet
another country side trip, see page 129). Soon you will enter Velarde,
which, along with Dixon and Embudo, is one of many small villages in
this fruit-growing area of the state. People don't think of New Mexicans
as fruit producers, but we are. Apricots, peaches, apples and raspberries
are the main crops. The seasonal roadside stands sell many varieties of
fruit, jams and *ristras* (wreathes or strands of chile) as well as pottery
and other colorful items.

http://www.espanolaonline.com/
(Española on line)

http://www.espanolanmchamber.com/tours/tour1.asp
(Española Valley Chamber of Commerce)
http://www.town.espanola.on.ca/Community/chistory.htm
(History of Española)
http://www.nmohwy.com/e/espanola.htm
(Española, NM)

Towns along the River

Further up the road, you'll pass Embudo Station. During the summer months, a lovely restaurant on the other side of the river specializes in brewed beer and barbecue. Right outside of Embudo you'll see a classic Hispanic country cemetery. Just beyond, at the Rió Grande Gorge Visitors Center, you can stop for information about the route and available activities, mainly river rafting. During spring and summer, the river is filled with rafts and kayaks. Early spring runoff sometimes contains rushing rapids, but later, for the most part, the water is relatively calm, with some rough spots—"The Box," right above Taos, and "The Toilet Bowl," a dangerous whirlpool just below the village of Pilar. If you decide to go river rafting (see page 145), your guide can help you select the type of experience for you.

http://www.embudostation.com/embudo.htm
(Embudo Station)
http://www.knownworldguides.com/rio.html
(New Mexico River Adventures)

Further on up the road you come to the tiny village of Pilar, where many rafting trips commence. The road is fairly curvy at this point, and, after climbing upward you finally arrive at a plateau with a view that stretches our forever. From here you can see Mount Wheeler, at 13,161 feet, the highest peak in New Mexico.

http://www.newmexicoet.com/nm_things_1p04.html
(Pilar, New Mexico)
http://melx2.home.mindspring.com/hp/new_mexico.htm
(Wheeler Peak, New Mexico)

San Francisco de Assisi Village Church
N.M. 68, Rancho de Taos
(505) 758-2754

Shortly you'll approach Ranchos de Taos, a small village made famous by Georgia O'Keeffe, Ansel Adams, Paul Strand and others who captured with their artistic skills the adobe fortress that is the San

The San Francisco de Assisi Village Church in Ranchos de Taos has been a favorite subject of painters and photographers for almost two centuries.

Francisco de Assisi Village Church. The back of the church (not the front!) with its buttresses and undulating adobe has captivated painters and photographers alike. Built in 1815 by the Franciscans, the church is four miles south of Taos on N.M. 68. From here you can continue on into Taos.

http://www.nmmagazine.com/nmregions/ncranchosdetaos.html

(Ranchos de Taos)

http://www.smithsonianmag.si.edu/smithsonian/issues99/dec99/churches.html

("mudding" of the village church)

PLACES TO SEE WHILE IN TAOS

Keep in mind that simply doing the low and high road to Taos and back to Santa Fe can be an all-day excursion, depending on stops. Seeing all that Taos itself has to offer is in itself at least another full day of touring. We do recommend that you take a self-guided walking tour of downtown Taos, availing yourself as well of the art museums both in town and slightly out of town. You can buy a combination ticket for the walking tour or house tour, or a more inclusive ticket that includes the museums.

http://www.taosmuseums.org/

(Museum Association of Taos)

http://www.taosmuseums.org/tickets_map.php

(Combination Tickets—Museum Association of Taos)

Governor Bent House
117-A Bent Street
(505) 758-2376

As a result of the Mexican War in 1846, the United States annexed New Mexico. Charles Bent was then appointed the first Territorial governor. He married Maria Ignacia, the older sister of Josefa Jaramillo, wife of the legendary Kit Carson. Bent, a mountain man, trader and trapper, was killed and scalped in 117-A Bent Street by an angry mob protesting the U.S. annexation, less than a year after his appointment.

http://www.laplaza.org/art/museums_bent.php3
(Governor Bent House)

Ernest Blumenschein House
222 Ledoux Street
(505) 758-0505

In the early 1900s Blumenschein and fellow artist Bert Phillips were touring New Mexico from Chicago. The wheel on their wagon broke, and Bert volunteered to take it into the nearest town for repair. When he returned with the repaired wheel, he told Blumenschein that he had just discovered the ideal town in which to live and paint. These two became the first of the Eastern artists in Taos and were the beginning of the Taos Society of Artists. Dating back to 1797, this house will take you back in time to the peaceful, old Taos days.

http://www.nmculture.org/cgi-bin/instview.cgi?_recordnum=ELB
(E. L. Blumenschein House and Museum)
http://www.taosmuseums.org/blumenschein.php
(E. L. Blumenschein House and Museum)
http://www.taoshistoricmuseums.com/blumenschein.html
(E. L. Blumenschein House and Museum)

The Kit Carson House
one-half block from Taos Plaza on Kit Carson Road
(505) 758-4741

The house in which Kit and his wife, Josefa, lived for 25 years is filled with Indian artifacts and period furniture of the 1800s. Although a general in the Union Army, Kit was illiterate, not unusual in those days. Nonetheless, he had an amazing facility for languages and served as a translator for a wagon train to Chihuahua. A man of many talents, Kit

Carson served as a scout for the John C. Fremont expeditions, worked as an Indian agent and thereafter became a military officer.

http://www.ranchoarriba.com/kitcarson.htm
(The Kit Carson Museum)

http://www.taoshistoricmuseums.com/kit_carson.html
(Kit Carson Home and Museum)

http://www.nmculture.org/cgi-bin/instview.cgi?_recordnum=KCM
(Kit Carson Historic Museums, Administrative Offices)

Kit Carson Memorial State Park
Paseo del Pueblo Norte at Civic Plaza
(505) 758-8234
Open every day 8 A.M.–8 P.M in warm weather;
9 A.M.–5 P.M. in the winter

This lovely park is home to many local outdoor events, including the annual Taos Solar Music Festival. It also houses recreational activities and a small cemetery. Buried here are Mabel Dodge Lujan, Padre Antonio José Martinez—who was always at odds with Archbishop Lamy—and, or course, Kit and Josefa Carson.

http://www.mabeldodgeluhan.com/
(The Mabel Dodge Lujan House)

http://www.findagrave.com/cgi-bin/fg.cgi?page=gr&GRid=9648
(Padre Antonio José Martinez)

http://www.solarmusicfest.com/index.shtml
(Taos Solar Music Festival)

E. I. Couse Home & Studio
146 Kit Carson Road
(505) 751-0369 or (505) 737-0105
Open May–October

E.I. Couse was one of the six founding artists of the Taos Society of Artists. The house, designated a National Trust Associate Site in 2002, stands as a testament to the beginnings of Taos as an American art colony. It houses the original furnishings and Couse's collection of Indian artifacts.

http://www.collectorsguide.com/ts/tsfa13.shtml
(E.I. Couse Home & Studio)

http://www.saginawimages.org/essay.asp?ItemID=SMES0005&SearchTerm=174
(about E.I. Couse)

Harwood Foundation Museum and Library
238 Ledoux Street
(505) 758-9826

With its exhibition program and its growing permanent collection, the fascinating Harwood Museum serves as a valuable resource for the Northern New Mexico region. It also provides a research facility for many scholars, educators, authors and students. If you'd like to see more representations of the Taos Society of Artists, then head up the street to the Harwood.

http://harwoodmuseum.org/harwood.php
(The Harwood Museum)

Mabel Dodge Luhan House
Historic Inn and Conference Center
240 Morada Lane
(800) 846-2235 or (505) 751-9686

During the 1920s wealthy socialite Mabel Dodge Lujan and her husband, Tony, from Taos Pueblo, constructed a large airy home surrounding a small dark adobe building now over 200 years old. Los Gallos, as the home was named, came to represent a conjunction between an elite world of artists and philosophers and one of the most enduring Native societies in the U.S. Guests over the years included Emma Goldman, Alfred Stieglitz, Margaret Sanger, John Reed and others of the political and artistic avant-garde. Other famous visitors included Georgia O'Keeffe, Willa Cather, Ansel Adams and Carl Jung. Actor Dennis Hopper owned the house briefly in the '70s, and his guests included Bob Dylan, Alan Watts and George McGovern. In 1991 the Mabel Dodge Luhan House was designated a National Historic Landmark and is now open to the public as a bed-and-breakfast, retreat and conference center.

http://www.mabeldodgeluhan.com
Mabel Dodge Luhan House

Martinez Hacienda
Off Highway 68 at Ranchos de Taos, then left on N.M. 240 for 3 miles
(505) 758-1000

Built between 1804 and 1827, this hacienda served as a fortress against Indian raids. Severino Martinez, both trader and farmer, was the builder. Traders using the Camino Real (Royal Road) unloaded goods

Visit the Martinez Hacienda for an authentic glimpse into
what life was like during the colonial period.

in Santa Fe (see pages x, 17 and 29) and then headed to Taos and the
Martinez Hacienda, their last stop. Its restored rooms display furniture,
crafts and food of the period and will give you genuine insight into life
during that time.

http://www.taoshistoricmuseums.com/martinez.html

(La Hacienda de los Martinez)

http://www.taosmuseums.org/hac_martinez.php

(La Hacienda de los Martinez)

Rió Grande Gorge Bridge

From N.M. 68, make a left onto U.S. 64 and go west to the bridge.

We've all seen bridges, but you shouldn't miss this one. It's the second-
highest expansion bridge in the country! In fact, standing on it and
looking into the awesome gorge far below can bring on vertigo. If
you've got the energy, hike down the path into the gorge, or hike at
least some of the way down. Make sure you have a hat, sunglasses,
plenty of water and, of course, wear hiking boots.

http://sangres.com/statenm/riogrgorge.htm

(Rió Grande Gorge Bridge)

http://www.evanderputten.org/special/newmexico/rgbridge.htm

(Rió Grande Gorge)

**http://www.rozylowicz.com/visitors/rio-grande-gorge-bridge-
panorama.html**

(panoramic view of Gorge Bridge)

The Rió Grande Gorge provides one of the
most spectacular views in the Southwest.

The Millicent Rogers Museum

1504 Museum Road (BA 030)

(505) 758-2462

Millicent Rogers (1902-1953) was the granddaughter of one of the original founders of Standard Oil, Henry Huttleston Rogers. She lived much
of her life in Europe but was drawn to the beauty and history of Taos,
and she began collecting Indian and Hispanic art and crafts. Her collection, encompassing well over 5,000 pieces, includes María Martínez
pottery as well as rugs, blankets, jewelry, Kachinas, paintings and religious objects. The museum is extraordinary and shows you what can
happen when people who have money also have passion and good taste
and love collecting. The site itself is breathtaking for its mountain and
high desert vistas.

http://www.millicentrogers.com/
(The Millicent Rogers Museum)
http://www.napoleonseries.org/genealogy/10724.htm
(Millicent Mary Henriette Rogers)
http://www.collectorsguide.com/ts/tsfa10.html
(Millicent Rogers Museum)

Taos Art Museum at the Fechin House
227 Paseo del Pueblo Norte
(505) 758-2690

The Russian artist, architect and sculptor Nicolai Fechin lived here from 1927 to 1933. The building is a monument to the architectural marriage of an adobe house and a Russian interpretation of corbels, beams and windows. The Taos Art Museum, featuring the works of the Taos Society of Artists, moved to this space in 2003.

http://www.taosartmuseum.org/
(Taos Art Museum)
http://www.fryeart.org/fechin/fechinmain.html
(Nicolai Fechin)
http://www.fechin.com/
(Fechin Art Workshops)

Taos Pueblo
Off N.M. 68
(505) 758-1028

We'll talk more of this ancient pueblo in the next chapter, but once you're in Taos this is a place you need to see. Said to be over 1,000 years old, it is the last surviving multi-storied pueblo. Although the Taos Pueblo people live in the modern world, they are still deeply tied to their culture and their religion, and they are sacredly bound to never reveal the details of either. Ansel Adams and other photographers were deeply touched by the architecture of the pueblo and by its people. Crafts and food are available and for sale.

http://taospueblo.com/
(Taos Pueblo)
http://www.newmexico.org/culture/pueblo_taos.html
(Taos Pueblo schedule and contacts)
http://www.8northern.org/taos.php
(Taos Pueblo)

THE PUEBLOS

Any trip to New Mexico and Santa Fe would hardly be complete without a seeing at least one pueblo in the area. A visit to a pueblo, especially during a feast day when dances take place, is to truly absorb the culture and flavor of ancient times and the Southwest. Feast days are open to the public (see page 191).

If you wish, you can gamble at one of the many flourishing pueblo casinos. These have been established to raise money for the tribes, and they have provided jobs as well as funds for essential services such as health centers, schools and college scholarships. Some of the casinos have expanded to include nightclub acts and hotels.

In the introduction to her book, *Pueblo People*, Marcia Keegan provides a succinct introduction to the pueblos:

> *The Pueblo people of New Mexico live today in nineteen autonomous villages scattered over the northern half of the state. "Pueblo" is the Spanish word for village or town, and sixteenth century Spanish explorers first referred to these community dwellers as Pueblo Indians. At that time there may have been as many as eighty such villages throughout the region. Pueblo Indians of today, as well as the village-dwelling Hopi Indians of northern Arizona, are sovereign nations that trace their ancestries through various groups of early cultures that inhabited the American Southwest long before the nomadic Navajo or Apache Indians migrated into the region. Pueblo Indians do not have a common language, but are divided into five linguistic groups. Most, however, are bilingual, speaking English as well as their native tongues.*

Left: Comanche dancers at San Ildefonso Pueblo.

Early efforts to stamp out their religions were resisted by the
Pueblo people, and the Pueblos today practice a unique blend of
Christian and Native religions. A central feature of each pueblo is
a mission church; some of the churches date back to the seven-
teenth century, when they were constructed under the supervision
of Franciscan friars. Native religion and culture find expression
today in the traditional ceremonial dances performed on the spa-
cious open plaza in the center of each pueblo. Many of the annual
feast day ceremonial dances are open to the public. Rituals of the
traditional Pueblo religion are private and take place in enclosed
chambers called kivas.

Traditional Pueblo government, which has existed for many
centuries, is the most enduring form of local government in
America. Each pueblo has its own self-governing body and offi-
cials, and is represented in the All Indian Pueblo Council."
(Keegan, p. 11)

THE INDIAN PUEBLO CULTURAL CENTER

2401 Twelfth Street NW (1 block north of I-40)
Albuquerque, New Mexico 87192
(505) 843-7270
(800) 766-4405 outside of New Mexico
Open daily 9:00 A.M.–5:30 P.M.
Museum hours: 9:00 A.M.–4:30 P.M.
Gift Shop hours: 9:00 A.M.–5:30 P.M.
The Pueblo Restaurant: 8:00 A.M–3:00 P.M.
Discount Pueblo Smoke Shop: 7 A.M.–6:30 P.M.
Indian Pueblo Cultural Center admission: free
Museum admission: $4 per person, seniors $3, students $1,
children 8 and up $1 and under 7 free with adult

A good introduction to the Pueblo Indians is the Indian Pueblo
Cultural Center. If you fly into Albuquerque, you can visit before heading north to Santa Fe.

Owned and operated by the nineteen Indian pueblos of New Mexico,
the Indian Pueblo Cultural Center showcases to more than 200,000 visitors each year the history and accomplishments of the Pueblo people,
from Pre-Columbian to current time. Its central focus is a 10,000-sqare-
foot museum that presents authentic history and artifacts of traditional

Zuni Olla women dancing at the Indian Pueblo Cultural Center. The ollas are the large pots they balance on their heads. You can see a variety of dances at the center.

Pueblo cultures as well as their contemporary art. The permanent exhibit highlights the creativity and adaptation that made possible the survival, diversity and achievements of each of the nineteen Pueblos. Also featured is a small, changing exhibit that highlights the work of living traditional and contemporary artists, usually those who conduct demonstrations at the center.

Traditional dances and festivals that form the centerpiece of Pueblo Indian spiritual and cultural life are performed in the courtyard. Performers from the nineteen New Mexico pueblos, from other Indian tribes and from other parts of the world are all drawn to the center, where they dance and represent a unique opportunity for visitors to see cultural diversity at one place. Dances are often impromptu affairs and can prove an exciting surprise to the unsuspecting visitor. They are scheduled regularly twice a day on Saturdays and Sundays.

http://www.indianpueblo.org/
(Indian Pueblo Cultural Center)

The pueblos are not only fascinating for their art and their history, but they are mythical places to many people. A case in point is the experience of C. G. Jung, the psychoanalyst, whose thinking transformed modern psychology and who was greatly influenced by a visit to Taos Pueblo.

In 1925, Jung spent time at Taos Pueblo and met Taos elder Ochwiay Biano (Mountain Lake). The perceptions Jung came away with from this meeting made a powerful impression on him and helped frame his conception of the psyche. He also witnessed how the Taos people retained age-old sacred rituals, which they kept secret to themselves and which gave them a connection with the mythic, archetypical, spiritual world. Jung wrote in his autobiography, *Memories, Dreams, Reflections*, "Preservation of secret traditions gives the Pueblo Indian pride and the power to resist the dominant whites. It gives them cohesion and unity; and I feel sure that the Pueblos as individual communities will continue to exist as long as their mysteries are not desecrated." (Jung, p. 250)

Jung also quoted Mountain Lake in his book, "We are a people who live on the roof of the world; we are the sons of Father Sun, and with our religion we daily help our father to go across the sky. We do this not only for ourselves, but for the whole world." (Jung, p. 252)

http://www.8northern.org/
(Eight Northern Indian Pueblos Council)
http://www.nmculture.org/cgi-bin/instview.cgi?_recordnum=BAND
(Bandelier National Monument)
http://www.newmexico.org/ScenicAttractions/ancientruins.html
(Ancient Ruins in New Mexico)
http://www.cinprograms.org/
(Council of Indian Nations)
http://www.geocities.com/Athens/9479/pueblo.html
(New Mexico Pueblos – Language)

PUEBLO ETIQUETTE

When visiting foreign countries it's appropriate to observe their rules and customs. The same courtesies apply when you visit the pueblos of Northern New Mexico. Some pueblos have fees for admission and for photography. In most instances, photography of dances and feast-day celebrations is prohibited. Some activities are closed to the public, and this needs to be respected. Here is a list to use as a guide:

- Please observe all rules and regulations of the individual pueblos.
- All homes at each pueblo are private. Never enter without an invitation.
- Please guide your children and see that they are respectful.
- Climbing walls or other structures is not permitted. Remember that some walls are several hundred years old and could be easily damaged.
- Removing any artifacts or objects, such as pieces of broken pottery, is forbidden.
- Please do not enter any kivas or graveyards.
- Alcohol, weapons and drugs are not tolerated.
- No pets are allowed.
- All Pueblo dances are religious ceremonies, not staged performances, and must be attended with respect.
- During the dances, please do not interrupt non-dancers' concentration by talking or waving to friends.
- Please do not talk to the dancers.
- No applause after dances, please.

http://www.8northern.org/etiquette.php
(Pueblo Etiquette)

Visiting a Pueblo Home

Entering a pueblo home is by invitation only. It is polite to accept an invitation to eat, but do not linger at the table as your host will be serving many guests throughout the day. Extend your thanks, but know that a payment is not appropriate.

Photography

Please contact each pueblo regarding permits, fees and restrictions concerning photography. Photographs are for your private use only. Ask permission before taking someone's photograph.

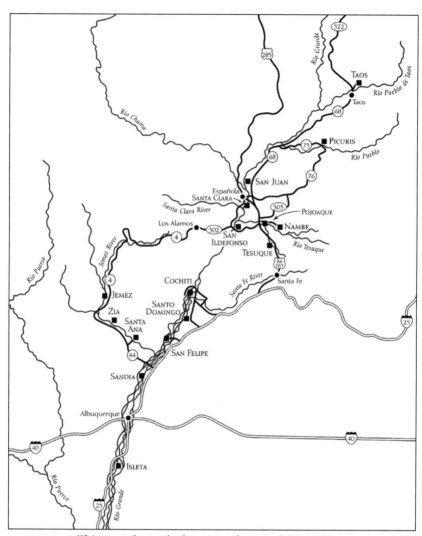

This map shows the location of most of the pueblos.
Acoma, Laguna and Zuni are located out west on I-40.
Map from *Pueblo People* ©Clear Light Publishing.

Which pueblo should I visit?

This book was designed to appeal to the visitor with limited time.
There are nineteen pueblos across Northern New Mexico—more pueblos than you'll have time to explore. Eight of these pueblos are within
easy driving distance of Santa Fe, with a drive time of between 30 minutes to 1½ hours drive time (Taos, combine with trip to Taos). We
suggest that you check out the feast days and choose to visit those
pueblos that mesh with your schedule in Santa Fe.

EIGHT NORTHERN INDIAN PUEBLOS

Located north of Santa Fe, these pueblos have for years been working together to create economic opportunities that benefit both themselves and the surrounding communities. Every summer, they put on one of the finest Indian arts and crafts shows in the country, the Eight Northern Indian Pueblos Council Artists and Craftsmen Show. The show is held the third week of July at the Eight Northern Indian Pueblos Indian Arts and Crafts Center at San Juan Pueblo. This is a wonderful opportunity for you to visit a pueblo and purchase some of the finest Indian arts and crafts directly from the artists at prices considerably lower than retail. For details on this year's show, call (800) 793-4955 or visit their Web site.

http://www.8northern.org/
(Eight Northern Indian Pueblos)

Nambé Pueblo
(505) 455-2036
Distance from Santa Fe: 17 miles

Nambé Pueblo is 12 miles north of Santa Fe on U.S. 84/285. Just after Pojoaque, turn right on N.M. 503. The pueblo is about four miles off N.M. 503, down a side road.

The best time to visit this small pueblo is on its major feast day, October 4, celebrating the Vespers of St. Francis of Assisi Day. Also of interest are the Nambé waterfalls and a lake that supplies water for the surrounding farmland.

http://www.8northern.org/nambe.php
(Nambé Pueblo)
http://www.newmexico.org/culture/pueblo_nambe.html
(Pueblo of Nambé)
http://www.nmmagazine.com/features/nambe.html
(Native Americans: Nambé Pueblo)
http://www.indianpueblo.org/ipcc/nambepage.htm
(Nambé Pueblo)

Picuris Pueblo
(505) 587-2519
Distance from Santa Fe: 60 miles

These Picuris dancers are performing the Belt Dance at the Hotel Santa Fe,
which is owned and operated by their Pueblo.

Go north on U.S. 84/285 from Santa Fe, then take N.M. 68 out of Española. At Embudo, turn onto N.M. 75.

Picuris is the smallest, most highly elevated (7,324 feet) and the most physically isolated of the nineteen pueblos. The Picuris Indians are the majority owners of one of Santa Fe's finest hotels—the Hotel Santa Fe—that status offering a viable future income to the residents of the pueblo (see page 103).

The feast day on August 10 commemorates the Pueblo Revolt against Spanish occupation, which occurred on August 10, 1680.

http://www.8northern.org/picuris.php
(Pueblo of Picuris)
http://www.newmexico.org/culture/pueblo_picuris.html
(Pueblo of "Picas." Picuris Pueblo)
http://www.nmmagazine.com/features/picuris.html
(Native Americans: Picuris Pueblo)
http://www.hotelsantafe.com/
(Hotel Santa Fe)
http://www.indianpueblo.org/ipcc/picurispage.htm
(Picuris Pueblo)

Pojoaque Pueblo
(505) 455-2278
Distance from Santa Fe: 15 miles

Pojoaque Pueblo is 15 miles north of Santa Fe just off U.S. 84/285.

The original name of this Pueblo is *Po-suwae-geh*, or "water drinking place." In fact, the pueblo was a place for travelers to stop and shop.

The main attraction here is the Poeh Cultural Center and Museum, which also has a gift shop and artist studios. The feast day, December 12, celebrates Our Lady of Guadalupe. Near the pueblo you'll find the Cities of Gold Casino (see also page 189).

http://towa.local.vm-net.com/cgi-bin/ PgOut.cgi?filename=PuebloHistory.html
(introduction and history of Pojoaque Pueblo)
http://www.8northern.org/pojoaque.php
(Pojoaque Pueblo)
http://www.newmexico.org/culture/pueblo_pojoaque.html
(Pueblo of Pojoaque)
http://www.nmmagazine.com/features/pojoaque.html
(Native Americans: Pojoaque Pueblo)
http://www.indianpueblo.org/ipcc/pojoaquepage.htm
(Pojoaque Pueblo)
http://www.citiesofgold.com/
(Cities of Gold Casino)
http://www.poehcenter.com/
(Poeh Cultural Center)

San Ildefonso Pueblo
(505) 455-2273
Distance from Santa Fe: 25 miles

Take U.S. 84/285 north. Just after passing Pojoaque, pick up N.M. 502 heading towards Los Alamos. Continue for 7 miles to the San Ildefonso turn-off.

One cannot visit this pueblo without feeling the presence of María Martínez and her son Julian, who developed the "black on black" pottery in 1919. To own a "Maria pot" is to own something beautiful and quite valuable. It is therefore not unusual that many of the inhabitants of this pueblo are potters and have been so for many generations. In addition San Ildefonso has artisans who specialize in paintings, silver jewelry, embroidery and moccasins. The pueblo feast day is January 23, when Comanche, Buffalo and Deer Dances are held.

http://www.newmexico.org/culture/pueblo_sanildefonso.html
(Pueblo of San Ildefonso)
http://www.nmmagazine.com/features/ildefonso.html
(Native Americans: San Ildefonso Pueblo)
http://www.edd.state.nm.us/FILM/PHOTOGALLERY/sanildefonso_pueblo.htm
(New Mexico Film Office Photo Gallery)
http://www.indianpueblo.org/ipcc/sanildefonsopage.htm
(San Ildefonso Pueblo)

San Juan Pueblo
(505) 852-4400
Distance from Santa Fe: 36 miles

Drive north of Santa Fe on U.S. 84/285. When you arrive in Española, follow the signs to stay on 285.

Historically this pueblo is most interesting. Don Juan de Oñate, a Spanish colonizer, came here from Mexico in 1598 with plans to erect a major city. San Juan Pueblo was, in fact, the predecessor of Santa Fe and was renamed San Juan de los Caballeros to replace the Indian name *Ohkay Owingeh*.

The San Juan Pueblo feast day is held on June 24 to honor St. John the Baptist, the patron saint of the pueblo. Buffalo and Comanche dances are held on the feast days.

The pueblo operates one of the largest casinos in New Mexico, the Ohkay Casino-Resort (see page 189).

http://www.8northern.org/sanjuan.php
(San Juan Pueblo)
http://www.newmexico.org/culture/pueblo_sanjuan.html
(Pueblo of San Juan)
http://www.nmmagazine.com/features/juan.html
(Native Americans: San Juan Pueblo)
http://www.indianpueblo.org/ipcc/sanjuanpage.htm
(San Juan Pueblo)
http://www.ohkay.com/
(Ohkay Casino-Resort)

Crucita Atencio of San Juan Pueblo winnowing corn.

Santa Clara Pueblo

(505) 753-7326
Distance from Santa Fe: 34 miles

Drive north on U.S. 84/285. In Española take NM 201, and then go one mile southwest on N.M. 30. The people of Santa Clara can trace their ancestry to the occupants of a cliffside village known as the Puye Cliff Dwellings. The stunning ruins were built alongside a cliff face in the Santa Clara Canyon and are open to visitors year round. In the 1500s, severe drought forced them to move into the valley of the Rió Grande, where the pueblo thrives today. Pottery is their main craft, and they are famous for their highly polished Blackware and Redware hand-coiled pots.

There are two feast days—June 13 and August 12—the "Big Feast" where Harvest, Blue Corn and other dances are performed. Santa Clara Pueblo owns the Black Mesa Golf Club, and it operates a casino and bowling alley, Big Rock Casino, in the middle of Española (see page 188).

http://www.8northern.org/santaclara.php
(Santa Clara Pueblo)
http://www.newmexico.org/culture/pueblo_santaclara.html
(Pueblo of Santa Clara)
http://www.nmmagazine.com/features/clara.html
(Native Americans: Santa Clara Pueblo)

http://www.indianpueblo.org/ipcc/santaclarapage.htm
(Santa Clara Pueblo)
http://www.gamblingmagazine.com/articles/07/07-296.htm
(article about Big Rock Casino Bowl)
http://www.blackmesagolfclub.com/
(Black Mesa Golf Club)
http://www.bigrockcasino.com/
(Big Rock Casino Bowl)

Taos Pueblo
(505) 758-1028
Distance from Santa Fe: 65 miles

Multi-storied Taos Pueblo still looks very much like it did centuries ago.

Drive north on US 84/285 then Highway 68. Go straight through the town of Taos. The pueblo is 2.7 miles north of Taos itself.

Taos Pueblo, or, "the Place of the Red Willows," sells both traditional and contemporary arts and crafts. Oven bread and traditional foods are also available.

The pueblo is open to tourists daily from 9 A.M. to 5 P.M.with fees for visiting and photographing. The feast days are May 3 (traditional foot races and Corn Dances); June 13, July 25 and 26 (Santiago's Day); September 30 (The Feast of San Geronimo). Taos also has a casino, Taos Mountain Casino (see page 190).

http://taospueblo.com/
(Taos Pueblo)

http://www.newmexico.org/culture/pueblo_taos.html
(Pueblo of Taos)
http://www.nmmagazine.com/features/taos.html
(Native Americans: Taos Pueblo)
http://www.indianpueblo.org/ipcc/taospage.htm
(Taos Pueblo)
http://taosmountaincasino.com/About.html
(Taos Pueblo)
http://www.taosmountaincasino.com/
(Taos Mountain Casino)

Tesuque Pueblo
(505) 983-2667
Distance from Santa Fe: 9 miles

Drive north on U.S. 84/285. Turn right at the sign for Tesuque.

The original pueblo existed before the year 1200, east of the current village. The current pueblo was re-established in 1694, soon after the Pueblo Revolt of 1680.

The annual feast day at the pueblo is on November 12 and commemorates San Diego. There is also a Corn Dance in June. Pueblo artists are in abundance, and many will sell artwork from their homes.

The casino here is Camel Rock (see page 188). The pueblo also runs the Tesuque Pueblo Flea Market as described on page 54.

http://www.8northern.org/tesuque.php
(Tesuque Pueblo)
http://www.newmexico.org/culture/pueblo_tesuque.html
(Pueblo of Tesuque)
http://www.nmmagazine.com/features/tesuque.html
(Native Americans: Tesuque Pueblo)
http://www.indianpueblo.org/ipcc/tesuquepage.htm
(Tesuque Pueblo)
http://www.camelrockcasino.com/
(Camel Rock Casino)

PUEBLOS SOUTH OF SANTA FE

In addition to the eight northern pueblos, there are eleven pueblos south of Santa Fe. All are quite interesting, so I'll leave it up to you. One mitigating factor is the amount of time you have in Santa Fe. Of course, there's always another visit to New Mexico, or, if you have come to Santa Fe by way of Albuquerque, you will find several on your way back or just slightly out of the way once there.

Acoma Pueblo
(505) 552-6604
Distance from Santa Fe: 132 miles

Acoma is known as "Sky City" because of its strategic clifftop location.

To get to Acoma Peublo, drive west from Albuquerque on I-40 (60 miles) and then 12 miles south on Indian Route 23 (exit 108).

Acoma, one of the most famous pueblos, is the oldest continuously inhabited city in the United States. It was built on top of a 357-foot sandstone mesa for defensive purposes over a thousand years ago. In a pitched battle against the Spanish troops of Juan de Oñate, the pueblo was nearly destroyed. Later, in a spiritually related conciliatory gesture, the Spanish mission of San Esteban del Rey Mission was built and completed in 1640. Guided tours are available. The pueblo also runs the Sky City Casino.

http://www.puebloofacoma.org/
(Acoma Pueblo)

http://www.indianpueblo.org/ipcc/acomapage.htm
(Acoma Pueblo)
http://www.nmculture.org/cgi-bin/instview.cgi?_recordnum=ACOM
(Acoma Pueblo Museum)
http://www.saveamericastreasures.org/profiles/sanesteban.htm
(San Esteban del Rey Mission)
http://www.skycitycasino.com/
(Sky City Casino)

Cochiti Pueblo
(505) 465-2244
Distance from Santa Fe: 27 miles

To reach Cochiti Pueblo, drive 22 miles south from Santa Fe on I-25. Exit at N.M. 16 and go another 14 miles.

The inhabitants of Cochiti Pueblo are famous for their handmade ceremonial drums as well as the storyteller ceramic figures originally created by the late Helen Cordero in 1964. These figures are now world-famous. You can also swim and boat at Cochiti Lake, where summer events are periodically held, or play golf at the 18-hole championship course nearby.

http://www.newmexico.org/culture/pueblo_cochiti.html
(Pueblo of Cochiti)
http://www.nmmagazine.com/features/cochiti.html
(Native Americans: Cochiti Pueblo)
http://www.indianpueblo.org/ipcc/cochitipage.htm
(Cochiti Pueblo)
http://livingtreasures.kxx.com/bios/helen.html
(Helen Cordero, Storyteller Creator)
http://www.collectorsguide.com/fa/fa014.shtml
(The First Storyteller)

Isleta Pueblo
(505) 869-3111
Distance from Santa Fe: 73

To get to Isleta Pueblo, drive 13 miles south of Albuquerque on I-25 and turn right off exit 215.

Isleta—"little island" in Spanish—was established in the 1300s. St. Augustine Church, built in 1612 and located on the main plaza, is fascinating historically and boasts traditional architecture. The pueblo operates the Isleta Casino & Resort, one of the largest pueblo casinos (see page 189).

http://www.isletapueblo.com/
(Pueblo of Isleta)
http://www.newmexico.org/culture/pueblo_isleta.html
(Pueblo of Isleta)
http://www.nmmagazine.com/features/isleta.html
(Native Americans: Isleta Pueblo)
http://www.indianpueblo.org/ipcc/isletapage.htm
(Isleta Pueblo)
http://www.isletacasinoresort.com/
(Isleta Casino & Resort)

Jemez Pueblo
(505) 834-7235
Distance from Santa Fe: 67 miles

To reach Jemez Pueblo, drive south on I-25 to the Cuba exit, and continue for 27 miles on U.S. 550.

Jemez combined with the Pecos Pueblo in 1838, when the people from the Pueblo of Pecos (located east of Santa Fe) resettled at the Pueblo of Jemez in order to escape the increasing depredations of the Spanish and Comanche cultures. They were rapidly integrated into Jemez society, and in 1936, both cultural groups were legally merged into one by an act of Congress. Today, the Pecos culture still survives at Jemez (see also page 137). The pueblo village, Walatowa, is only open to visitors on feast days, so call ahead for feast-day dates. Their visitor center, however, is always open and displays a reconstructed Jemez field house and other cultural exhibits as well as a gift shop.

http://www.jemezpueblo.org/
(Jemez Pueblo)
http://www.newmexico.org/culture/pueblo_jemez.html
(Pueblo of Jemez)
http://www.indianpueblo.org/ipcc/jemezpage.htm
(Pueblo of Jemez)

Laguna Pueblo
(505) 552-6654
Distance from Santa Fe: 105 miles

The dramatic skyline of Laguna Pueblo is visible from I-40.

Laguna Pueblo lies 45 miles west of Albuquerque off I-40 and 31 miles east of Grants.

Laguna Pueblo was named after a lake that has since disappeared from the area. The Pueblo and its famous mission church—San José de Laguna—were founded in 1699 by refugees from Cochiti and Santo Domingo at the end of the Pueblo Revolt. It has a population of about 7,700, making it one of the largest Keresan pueblos.

Pottery and other crafts are for sale all year, but the September 19 Feast of St. Joseph generally has hundreds of booths with crafts for sale. The pueblo operates the Dancing Eagle Casino, located on N.M. 114 (see page 189).

http://www.fourdir.com/keresan.htm
(Four Directions Institute – Keresan Pueblos)
http://web.nmsu.edu/~tomlynch/swlit.laguna-history.html
(Laguna Pueblo history)
http://web.nmsu.edu/~tomlynch/swlit.laguna.html
(Laguna Pueblo)
http://www.nmmagazine.com/features/laguna.html
(Native Americans: Laguna Pueblo)
http://www.indianpueblo.org/ipcc/lagunapage.htm
(Laguna Pueblo)
http://dancingeaglecasino.com/
(Dancing Eagle Casino)

Sandia Pueblo

(505) 867-3317
Distance from Santa Fe: 62 miles

The entrance to the casino at Sandia, one of the largest in the state.

To reach Sandia Pueblo, drive on I-25 to exit 235, and then about 12 miles to the pueblo.

This pueblo goes back to the 1300s. Originally named Nafiat ("dusty") it was given its modern name Sandia ("watermelon") by later Spanish colonists, who saw what they thought were watermelons growing in the pueblo. The Sandia Mountains were named after the pueblo. A large pueblo, it operates one of the biggest Native-owned arts-and-crafts markets in the Southwest, Bien Mur Indian Market, as well as one of the largest casinos, Sandia Casino. Both are located on the east side of I-25 off Tramway Boulevard (see page 190).

http://www.nmmagazine.com/features/sandia.html
(Native Americans: Sandia Pueblo)
http://www.sandiapueblo.nsn.us/sandia/
(Pueblo of Sandia)
http://www.indianpueblo.org/ipcc/sandiapage.htm
(Sandia Pueblo)
http://www.cs.unm.edu/~brayer/rock/sandia.html
(The Pueblo of Sandia Petroglyph Project)

http://www.bienmur.com/sandiapueblo.htm
(Sandia Pueblo NA-FIAT)
http://www.bienmur.com/
(Bien Mur Indian Market)
http://www.sandiacasino.com/
(Sandia Casino)

San Felipe Pueblo

(505) 867-3381
Distance from Santa Fe: 40 miles

San Felipe Pueblo is located 10 miles north of Bernalillo off I-25.

One of the most conservative of the pueblos, San Felipe was founded in the 1300s. The yearly highlight of the village is the celebration of the Feast of St. Philip on May 1. Then, hundreds of villagers do the beautiful and relentless Corn Dance. Crafts and jewelry are sold, especially during the arts-and-crafts show in October. Additionally, the tribe owns and operates the Casino Hollywood right off I-25 as well as the Hollywood Hills Speedway, where racing, outdoor events and concerts are held. (see page 189).

http://www.newmexico.org/culture/pueblo_sanfelipe.html
(Pueblo of San Felipe)
http://www.nmmagazine.com/features/felipe.html
(Native Americans: San Felipe Pueblo)
http://www.indianpueblo.org/ipcc/sanfelipepage.htm
(San Felipe Pueblo)
http://www.sanfelipecasino.com/
(Casino Hollywood)
http://www.hollywoodhillsspeedway.com/
(Hollywood Hills Speedway)

Santa Ana Pueblo

(505) 867-3301

Distance from Santa Fe: 45 miles

Santa Ana Pueblo's Hyatt Regency Tamaya Resort and Spa.

To get to Santa Ana Pueblo, take I-25 South to exit 242 and then drive 2 miles west to the intersection of U.S. 550 and N.M. 528 (Dove Road). The Santa Ana Pueblo people have occupied their current site in central New Mexico since at least the late 1500s. The original pueblo, at approximately 5,400 feet above sea level, lies against a mesa wall on the north bank of the Jemez River, a site providing protection and seclusion. For the most part travelers followed the north-south trade route along the Rió Grande or headed east and west; they made little contact, and as a result Santa Ana was seldom visited.

The pueblo is only open to the public on feast days. (January 1 and 6, as well as July 26, Santiago's Day).

The pueblo operates the Santa Ana and Twin Warriors Golf Clubs, the Santa Ana Garden Center, the highly prosperous Santa Ana Star Casino, and the new Hyatt Regency Tamaya Resort and Spa (see page 190).

http://www.santaana.org/

(The Pueblo of Santa Ana)

http://www.newmexico.org/culture/pueblo_santaana.html

(Pueblo of Santa Ana)

http://www.indianpueblo.org/ipcc/santaanapage.htm
(Santa Ana Pueblo)
http://www.nmmagazine.com/features/ana.html
(Native Americans: Santa Ana Pueblo)
http://www.doi.gov/plw/febmar2001/forest.htm
(Santa Ana Pueblo Restores Stretch of Rio Grande River)
http://www.santaanagolf.com/Santa_Ana/
(Santa Ana Golf Club)
http://www.twinwarriorsgolf.com/
(Twin Warriors Golf Club)
http://tamaya.hyatt.com/property/index.jhtml
(Tamaya Resort & Spa)
http://www.santaanastar.com/
(Santa Ana Star Casino)

Santo Domingo Pueblo

(505) 465-2214
Distance from Santa Fe: 25 miles

Drive south from Santa Fe on I-25. Santo Domingo is halfway between Santa Fe and Albuquerque.

Santo Domingo pueblo is located close to the old Cerrillos Hills turquoise mines. Is it any wonder that Santo Domingo Indians are skilled in the art of turquoise and *heishi* jewelry? The big annual event at the pueblo is the arts-and-crafts show held each Labor Day, but roadside stands selling jewelry as well as pottery are to be found in the pueblo year round. August 4 is the Feast of St. Dominic. This is the largest feast-day dance of all the pueblos, with thousands doing the traditional Corn Dance.

http://www.newmexico.org/culture/pueblo_santodomingo.html
(Pueblo of Santo Domingo)
http://www.nmmagazine.com/features/domingo.html
(Native Americans: Santo Domingo Pueblo)
http://www.indianpueblo.org/ipcc/santodomingopage.htm
(Santo Domingo Pueblo)

Zia Pueblo

(505) 867-3304
Distance from Santa Fe: 65 miles

To reach Zia Pueblo, drive south on I-25 from Santa Fe and then take the U.S. 550 exit. Go about 25 miles on U.S. 550 to the pueblo. This Keres-speaking pueblo is widely known for its ancient sun symbol and the thin-walled, Zia bird-symbol pottery. The sun symbol graphically depicts multiple stylized rays radiating in each of the four directions from a central sun. This symbol has been on the New Mexico flag since the 1920s. If you fly over the state Capitol in Santa Fe, you will see that the roof has a depiction of the sun symbol.

The Zia Cultural Center has pottery, sculpture and weavings for sale. The Feast Day honoring Our Lady of the Assumption takes place on August 15.

http://www.fourdir.com/keresan.htm
(Four Directions Institute – Keresan Pueblos)
http://www.nmmagazine.com/features/zia.html
(Native Americans: Zia Pueblo)
http://www.newmexico.org/culture/pueblo_zia.html
(Zia Pueblo)
http://www.indianpueblo.org/ipcc/ziapage.htm
(Zia Pueblo)
http://www.nmsu.edu/~bho/zia.html
(Zia Sun Symbol)

Zuni Pueblo

(505) 782-4403
Distance from Santa Fe: 180 miles

To get to Zuni Pueblo from Santa Fe, take I-25 to I-40 west. Look for the Zuni Pueblo exit (New Mexico 55), 35 miles before Gallup. Coronado, in his quest for gold, thought he had come upon one of the Seven Cities of Cibola when he entered the Zuni Pueblo. He found no gold, but today a visitor will find an abundance of turquoise and silver jewelry, including needle-point and inlay jewelry. The Zuni are the main carvers of fetishes—various stones carved into the likenesses of animals. Originally carved for hunters for protection and successful hunts, they are widely sought out by collectors around the world. Keshi, a store at 227 Don Gasper Avenue in Santa Fe, has had close ties with the pueblo since 1981, when it became a co-op for these beautiful carvings and other crafts (see page 114).

Zuni Buffalo Dancers.

Zuni is the most populated of all the pueblos. Its mission church, Our Lady of Guadalupe, built in 1629, contains some ten-foot Kachina murals painted by Alex Seowtewa. Call ahead for hours.

http://www.psi.edu/coronado/coronadosjourney2.html
(Coronado's Journey Through New Mexico, Texas, Oklahoma, and Kansas)
http://www.newmexico.org/culture/pueblo_zuni.html
(Pueblo of Zuni)
http://www.nmmagazine.com/features/zuni.html
(Native Americans: Zuni Pueblo)
http://www.indianpueblo.org/ipcc/zunipage.htm
(Zuni Pueblo)
http://www.keshi.com/
(Keshi: The Zuni Connection)

Our thanks to the New Mexico Department of Tourism for helping us to compile this section.

PUEBLO CASINOS

San Felipe Pueblo's Casino Hollywood.

Big Rock Casino Bowl
(505) 753-7326
Santa Clara Pueblo, distance from Santa Fe: 34 miles
Big Rock Casino Bowl includes bowling alley
http://www.bigrockcasino.com/
(Big Rock Casino Bowl)
http://www.gamblingmagazine.com/articles/07/07-296.htm
(article about Big Rock Casino Bowl)

Camel Rock Casino
(505) 983-2667
Tesuque Pueblo, distance from Santa Fe: 9 miles
Camel Rock Casino, Camel Rock Suites Hotel, The Rock Showroom
featuring national music acts and boxing
http://www.camelrockcasino.com/
(Camel Rock Casino)

Cities of Gold Casino
(505) 455-2278
Pojoaque Pueblo, distance from Santa Fe: 15 miles
Cities of Gold Casino, with sports bar featuring simulcast wagering,
Towa Golf Course, Cities of Gold Hotel and full-service restaurant,
Golden Cantina for drinks and live music
http://www.citiesofgold.com/
(Cities of Gold Casino)

Dancing Eagle Casino
(505) 552-6654
Laguna Pueblo, distance from Santa Fe: 105 miles
Dancing Eagle Casino, with restaurant and snack bar
http://dancingeaglecasino.com/
(Dancing Eagle Casino)

Isleta Casino & Resort
(505) 869-3111
Isleta Pueblo, distance from Santa Fe: 73 miles
Isleta Casino & Resort, several restaurants, national big-name music
acts, Isleta Eagle 27-hole championship golf course
http://www.isletacasinoresort.com/
(Isleta Casino & Resort)

Ohkay Casino-Resort
(505) 852-4400
San Juan Pueblo, distance from Santa Fe: 26 miles
Ohkay Casino-Resort, Best Western hotel, Ohkay Corral, 1,500-seat-
venue for rodeos and outdoor events and concerts
http://www.ohkay.com/
(Ohkay Casino-Resort)

San Felipe Casino Hollywood
(505) 867-3381
San Felipe Pueblo, distance from Santa Fe: 40 miles
San Felipe Casino Hollywood with Celebrity Showroom featuring
national music acts and Hollywood Hills Speedway, where auto racing,
outdoor events and concerts are held
http://www.sanfelipecasino.com/
(San Felipe Casino Hollywood)

Sandia Casino
(505) 867-3317
Sandia Pueblo, distance from Santa Fe: 62 miles
Sandia Casino with buffet dining
http://www.sandiacasino.com/
(Sandia Casino)

Santa Ana Star Casino
(505) 867-301
Santa Ana Pueblo, distance from Santa Fe: 45 miles
Santa Ana Star Casino, 3,000-seat arena with national acts, 45 holes championship golf (Twin Warriors & Santa Ana Golf), Starlight Lanes bowling, arcade games
http://www.santaanastar.com/
(Santa Ana Star Casino)

Sky City Casino
(505) 552-6017
Acoma Pueblo, distance from Santa Fe: 132 miles
Sky City Casino, Huwaka Restaurant, Sky City Hotel & Conference Center
http://www.skycitycasino.com/
(Sky City Casino)

Taos Mountain Casino
(505) 758-1028
Taos Pueblo, distance from Santa Fe: 65 miles
Taos Mountain Casino, featuring majestic views and live local music
http://taosmountaincasino.com/
(Taos Mountain Casino)

CALENDAR OF DANCES & FEAST DAYS

Please call prior to visiting any pueblo for changes and updates on events. See pages 165–187 for pueblo offices and phone numbers.

http://www.indianpueblo.org/index.cfm?module=ipcc&pn=17
(Indian Pueblo Cultural Center Calendar of Feast Days and Dances)

http://www.8northern.org/dances.php
(Pueblo Feast Days and Dances)

http://www.archdiocesesantafe.org/AboutASF/Parishes/PuebloFeasts.html
(Pueblo Annual Feast Days)

http://www.santaana.org/calendar.htm
(Calendar of Native American Events and Dances)

January 1
Dances at many pueblos, including Taos Pueblo—Turtle Dance
Santo Domingo Pueblo—Corn Dance
San Juan Pueblo—Cloud or Basket Dance

January 6
All pueblos:
King's Day celebrations and dances (annual transference of leadership)

January 22
San Ildefonso Pueblo—evening firelight procession

January 23
San Ildefonso Pueblo Feast Day—Buffalo, Comanche and Deer Dances

January 25
Picuris Pueblo—St. Paul's Feast Day

February 2
San Felipe and Picuris Pueblos—Candelaria Day Celebration

Late February
San Juan Pueblo—Deer Dances

March 19
Laguna Pueblo (Old Laguna)—St. Joseph's Feast Day,
Harvest Dance & various dances

Easter Weekend
Most pueblos—Basket and Corn Dances
Nambé Pueblo—Bow & Arrow Dance after Mass
Zia Pueblo—various dances Sunday and Monday
San Ildefonso—various dances

April 1
Jemez Pueblo—Open Air Market

May 1
San Felipe Pueblo Feast Day—Corn Dance

May 2
Cochiti Pueblo—Santa Cruz Feast Day and Corn Dance

May 3
Taos Pueblo—Santa Cruz Feast Day, Blessing of the Fields

Memorial Day Weekend
Jemez Pueblo—Red Rocks Arts & Crafts Show

June, first Saturday
Tesuque Pueblo—Blessing of the Fields, Corn Dance

June 13
Sandia Pueblo—San Antonio Feast Day
Taos and Picuris Pueblos—Corn Dances
Santa Clara Pueblo—Comanche Dance

June 24
San Juan Pueblo Feast Day—Buffalo and Comanche Dances
Taos Pueblo—Corn Dance

June 29
Santa Ana Pueblo—San Pedro Feast Day, Corn Dance

July, first weekend
Picuris Pueblo Arts and Crafts Fair

July 4
Mescalero Apaches—Maiden's Puberty Rites, Mountain Spirits Dance
Nambé Pueblo—Winter Buffalo, Spear, Yellow Corn, White Buffalo
and Comanche Dances

July, second weekend
Taos Pueblo Annual Pow-Wow

July 14
Cochiti Pueblo Feast Day

Mid July
Jicarilla Apaches—Little Beaver Roundup & Rodeo,
various dances, Dulce, N.M.
Eight Northern Indian Pueblos Annual Artists & Craftsmen Show
at San Juan Pueblo
http://www.8northern.org/arts.php
(Eight Northern Indian Pueblos Artists & Craftsmen Show)

July 25
Taos Pueblo—Santiago Feast Day, Corn Dance

July 26
Santa Ana Pueblo—Feast Day and Corn Dance
Taos Pueblo—Corn Dance
Laguna Pueblo (Seama)—St. Ann's Feast Day with Harvest
and various dances

August 2
Jemez Pueblo—Nuestra Señora de Los Angeles Feast Day

August 4
Santo Domingo Annual Feast Day, Corn Dance

August 9
Picuris Pueblo—San Lorenzo sunset dances

August 10
Acoma Pueblo (Acomita)—San Lorenzo Feast Day
Picuris Pueblo Feast Day—Ceremonial Foot Race, Pole Climb & dances

August 12
Santa Clara Pueblo Feast Day—Buffalo, Harvest or Corn Dance

Mid-August
Gallup Inter-Tribal Indian Ceremonial,
featuring 50 tribes in dances, rodeos, parades and arts-and-crafts at
Red Rock State Park near Gallup
http://www.gallupnm.org/ceremonial/
(Inter-Tribal Indian Ceremonial)

August 15
Zia Pueblo Annual Feast Day and Corn Dances
Laguna Pueblo (Mesita)—The Assumption of Our Blessed
Mother's Feast Day, Harvest and various dances

August 15–21
Zuni Pueblo—Annual Zuni Tribal Fair

Weekend following the third Thursday in August
SWAIA Annual Indian Market, Santa Fe
http://www.swaia.org/indianmrkt.html
(Indian Market)

August 28
Isleta Pueblo—St. Augustine Feast Day, Mass in the morning and a
procession following Mass, Indian dances in the afternoon

September, first weekend
Santo Domingo Pueblo Annual Arts & Crafts Show

September 2
Acoma Pueblo (Old Acoma Pueblo)—San Estevan Feast Day
and Harvest Dance

September 4
Isleta Pueblo—St. Augustine Feast Day and Harvest Dance

September 8
Laguna Pueblo (Encinal)—Nativity of the Blessed Virgin Mary's
Annual Feast Day, Harvest and social dances
San Ildefonso Pueblo—Corn Dance

Second or third weekend in September
Jicarilla Apaches—Stone Lake Fiesta, various dances in Dulce, N.M.

September 19
Laguna Pueblo (Old Laguna)—St. Joseph's Annual Feast Day with
Buffalo, Eagle and social dances

September 25
Laguna Pueblo (Paguate)—St. Elizabeth Annual Feast Day,
Harvest and social dances

September 29
Taos Pueblo—San Geronimo Eve, Vespers and sundown dance

September 30
Taos Pueblo—San Geronimo Feast Day, Ceremonial Foot Races
and Pole Climb

October 4
Nambé Pueblo—St. Francis de Assisi Feast Day, Buffalo
and Deer Dances

October 17
Laguna Pueblo (Paraje)—St. Margaret and Mary's Feast Day with
Harvest and social dances

November 12
Jemez Pueblo Feast Day
Tesuque Pueblo—San Diego Feast Day, various dances

November, last week
Zuni Pueblo—Christmas Light Parade

Late November or early December
Zuni Pueblo—Shalako Ceremonial

December, first weekend
Jemez Pueblo—Walatowa Winter Arts & Crafts Fair
Eight Northern Indian Pueblos Winter Arts & Crafts Fair
at San Juan Pueblo

December 11
Pojoaque Pueblo—Vespers and procession usually held at 6 p.m.

December 12
Pojoaque Pueblo Annual Feast Day—Mass at 10 a.m., dances per-
formed after Mass
Jemez, Santa Clara, and Tesuque Pueblos—various dances

December 24 and 25
Picuris Pueblo—Christmas celebration, Spanish dance drama
Los Matachines
San Juan Pueblo—Christmas celebration, Spanish dance drama *Los
Matachines*, Pine Torch Procession

December 24, Christmas Eve
Dances at most pueblos, some after midnight Mass
Taos Pueblo—Sundown Procession with Bonfires
Acoma Pueblo—*Luminarias*
Laguna Pueblo—Various Dances after 10:00 Mass
Santa Ana and Tesuque Pueblos—dances after midnight Mass,
Nambé Pueblo—Buffalo, Deer and Antelope Dances after Mass

December 25, Christmas Day
Tesuque Pueblo—various dances
Taos Pueblo—Deer or Spanish dance drama *Los Matachines*
San Ildefonso Christmas celebration—Spanish dance drama *Los
Matachines*

December 25–28
Laguna Pueblo—Harvest Dance

APPENDIX

MAJOR YEARLY EVENTS
& CELEBRATIONS

Here is a list of some events you may wish to attend while in Santa Fe. You will find more in the local papers when you arrive. See the previous pages for the calendar of major Indian events. To aid in planning, you can log on to the Santa Fe Convention and Visitors Bureau Web site, which has a detailed calendar for every month of the year, with descriptions of each event and links to their Web sites.

http://santafe.org/Calendar_of_Events/
(Santa Fe Convention and Visitors Bureau Calendar of Events)

Super Bowl Weekend
"Souper Bowl"
Fund-raiser for the Food Depot where you can sample soups from the best of Santa Fe restaurants (check local newspapers for details).

Good Friday
Pilgrimage to the Santuario de Chimayó
http://www.evanderputten.org/special/newmexico/chimayó.htm
(El Santuario de Chimayó)

First Tuesday in May
The Taste of Santa Fe
Sample the best dishes from the best Santa Fe
restaurants. Proceeds benefit the Palace of the Governors.

Summer Music
The **Santa Fe Chamber Music Festival, The Santa Fe Opera** and the
Santa Fe Desert Chorale all perform during the summer months.
Please see pages 46–49 for details.

Left: The burning of Zozobra, "Old Man Gloom," draws tens of thousands of cheering onlookers every year and welcomes in the start of the Fiesta de Santa Fe.

Early June
El Rancho de las Golondrinas Spring Festival and Annual Fair
(505) 471-2261
http://www.golondrinas.org/
(El Rancho de las Golondrinas)

Mid-June
Buckaroo Ball
Dinner, garden tours, brunch over a three-day period, charity event
(505) 992-3700
http://buckarooball.com/
(Buckaroo Ball)

Mid- to Late-June
Rodeo de Santa Fe
3237 Rodeo Road (at Richards Avenue and at Avenida Pueblos)
P.O. Box 5185, Santa Fe, NM 87502-5185
(505) 471-4300
$7 per person matinee, $8 evening ($1 less for kids and seniors)
http://www.rodeodesantafe.org/pages/1/index.htm
(Rodeo de Santa Fe)

Late June
Taos Solar Music Festival
eclectic music combined with solar-energy information booths
and handicrafts, Taos
http://www.solarmusicfest.com/index.shtml
(Taos Solar Music Festival)

July
Fourth of July Pancake Breakfast
Kiwanis Club Pancake Breakfast on the Plaza

Mid-July
El Rancho de las Golondrinas Wine Festival
Call for dates and directions—(505) 471-2261
http://www.golondrinas.org/julyevents.htm
(Santa Fe Wine Festival)

Last weekend in July
Spanish Market
Oldest and largest exhibition and sale of traditional Spanish
colonial artforms in the United States
http://www.spanishmarket.org/
(Spanish Market)

Late July
Eight Northern Indian Pueblos Council Artists & Craftsmen Show
For details on this year's show, call (800) 793-4955.
http://www.8northern.org/
(Eight Northern Indian Pueblos)

Late July
Behind Adobe Walls®
Garden tours sponsored by the Santa Fe Garden Club
(505) 982-0807 or (800) 732-6881

Mid-August
Lavender Fest at El Rancho de las Golondrinas
Products, plants and demonstrations
http://www.golondrinas.org/calendar.htm
(2003 Calendar of Events)

Mid- to Late-August
Santa Fe Bluegrass & Old-Time Music Festival
http://www.southwestpickers.org/festivals.html
(Santa Fe Bluegrass Festival)

Weekend following the third Thursday in August
SWAIA Santa Fe Indian Market
Probably the most well known of all Santa Fe events. Over 2,000
Indian artists from across the country show their work in this
famous Indian show on the Santa Fe Plaza.
http://www.swaia.org/indianmrkt.html
(Indian Market)
http://www.swaia.org/
(SWAIA—Southwestern Association of Indian Arts)

Late-August
Thirsty Ear Music Festival
A festival of blues, folk, alt-country and roots-rock artists
http://www.thirstyearfestival.com/
(Thirsty Ear Festival)

Early September, weekend after Labor Day
Fiestas de Santa Fe
A four-day event beginning with the burning of the three-story
puppet figure Zozobra, or "Old Man Gloom."
Festivities are continued on the Plaza and include the Pet Parade and
the Historical/Hysterical Parade. Mass and the Processional to the
Cross of the Martyrs conclude the Fiesta. (505) 988-7575.

The king and queen lead the Fiesta Parade around the Plaza.

http://www.santafefiesta.org/
(Santa Fe Fiesta Council)
http://www.zozobra.com/
(Burning of Zozobra)
http://www.zozobra.com/zhistory.html
(Zozobra history)
http://www.newmexico.org/Fun/crossmaryrs1.html
(Cross of the Martyrs, Santa Fe)

Late-September
Santa Fe Wine & Chile Fiesta
http://www.santafewineandchile.org/
(Santa Fe Wine & Chile Fiesta)

First Weekend in October
El Rancho de las Golondrinas Harvest Festival
http://www.golondrinas.org/octevents.htm
(Harvest Festival)

Mid-October
Santa Fe Jazz Festival
http://www.santafejazzfestival.com/
(Santa Fe Jazz Festival)

First Weekend in December
Winter Spanish Market
http://www.spanishmarket.org/
(Spanish Market)

Second Friday in December
Christmas at the Palace
Open house Friday evening at the Palace of the Governors
http://palaceofthegovernors.org/
(Palace of the Governors)

Third Sunday in December
Las Posadas Procession
In and around Santa Fe Plaza. Here, actors portraying Mary and Joseph try to find an inn for the night. An actor portraying the devil hovers on the rooftops overlooking the Plaza, making sure they will have no place to rest. Eventually, they're taken in at the Palace of the Governors. This performance is a must-see!

Christmas Eve
Canyon Road Walk
This informal walk seems to be taken by all of Santa Fe and is a delight. Homes and businesses on Canyon Road put up *farolitos* (paper bags weighted with sand with candle inserted) to light your way. Bonfires and music warm the body and soul.
http://www.santafenow.com/links/Dec/
(Christmas in Santa Fe)
http://www.desertusa.com/mag00/jul/stories/croad.html
(Canyon Road)
http://santafe.com/travel/kids.html
(Christmas and winter events in Santa Fe)

Christmas Day
Dances at most pueblos—see page 195.

WORDS & PHRASES
YOU'LL HEAR ABOUT TOWN

Acequia Madre—Mother Ditch. The word *acequia* is an old Arabic word adopted by the Spanish, meaning "canal." In New Mexico, these little canals are referred to as "ditches." *Madre* is the Spanish word for "mother"—hence, "Mother Ditch."

Anglo—any person not of Hispanic or Native American descent

Arroyo— a natural watercourse, usually dry (except after rainstorms)

Bajada—descent of a hill

Bulto—a statue, usually of a saint, made of carved cottonwood root

Calle—street

Canale—drain spout extending out from a parapet of a flat roof

Corbel—scroll-shaped wood bracket used to support a viga

Entrada—expedition or entryway

Gringo—an American, a foreigner, a "white man." One suggestion as to its origin goes that during the Mexican-American Wars, a popular song in the United States was "Green Grow the Lilacs." American soldiers sang it, and the Mexicans took the first two words, which sounded like "gringo" to them, and gave that name to the American soldiers.

Horno—outdoor oven

Latilla—branches used for ceilings and coyote fences

Parroquia—the parish church

Portal—a long covered porch supported by corbels on posts

Posada—inn

Retablo—a wooden panel painted with a religious image for use in churches

Ristra—a string of chiles

Santero—a carver of the saints

Santo—carved saint

Trastero—a wooden cupboard

Viga—a debarked log used as a ceiling beam

WORDS FOUND IN RESTAURANT MENUS

Here are some Spanish words that will help you get around town, order in a restaurant and just plain make you part of Santa Fe.

Carne adovada—pork stew marinated in red chile sauce, usually rich, hot and delicious

Chile—chile pepper, can be red or green

Chile "Christmas"—This does not refer to the December holiday but is frequently used in restaurants in town. Since all restaurants prepare chile differently, it's hard to know if green or red chile is the hotter or tastier. The best bet is to tell your server to bring "Christmas," which means half-green, half-red chile. Incidentally, you can always ask for your chile on the side, if you are not sure you want chile at all.

Chile rellenos—moderately hot chiles stuffed with cheese then dipped in egg batter and fried

Fajitas—a very tasty combination of stir-fried onions, green peppers, and chiles plus marinated steak, chicken or shrimp, served with warm flour tortillas and condiments

frijoles—beans

piñon—the nut of the piñon tree, used in many dishes and salads

sopaipillas—a classic New Mexican puffy flatbread that is deep fried and usually served with honey

tortilla—a round fried thin flatbread made of flour or ground yellow or blue corn meal

SOURCE NOTES

Clark, Edward C. "Chimayó." Unpublished manuscript, Santa Fe, 1995.

Cook, Mary Jean and Cordelia Snow. "Palace Walking Tour Historic Events." Docent brochure, Palace of the Governors, Santa Fe, 1997.

Grant, D.N. *Santa Fe: History of Our Ancient City.* Santa Fe: School of American Research Press, 1989.

Jung, C.G. *Memories, Dreams, Reflections.* Aniela Jaffé, editor. Richard and Clara Winston, translators. New York: Vintage Books (a division of Random House), 1989.

Keegan, Marcia. *Pueblo People: Ancient Traditions, Modern Lives.* Santa Fe: Clear Light Publishers, 1999.

La Farge, John Pen. *Turn Left at the Sleeping Dog.* Albuquerque: University of New Mexico Presss, 2001.

Lawrence, D.H. Essay, N.p., c. 1924.

"Palace of the Governors Lectures." Docent lecture series, Palace of the Governors, Santa Fe, 1999.

Poling-Kempes, Lesley. *Valley of the Shining Stone: The Story of Abiquiú.* Tucson: University of Arizona Press, 1997.

Simmons, Mark. Column, *Santa Fe New Mexican,* April 27, 2002.

Uhlenhopp, Jack. "Docent Notes on the Palace of the Governors." Oral transmission, Santa Fe, June 2002.

INDEX

Page numbers in bold indicate illustrations.